SHOP DRAWINGS
for
GREENE & GREENE FURNITURE

Robinson House dining room at the Huntington Museum, Los Angeles. The table is drawn on page 82 and the chairs on page 122.

Photo: Ognan Borissov, Interfoto

Shop Drawings
for
Greene & Greene Furniture

23 American Arts & Crafts Masterpieces

Measured and drawn by
Robert W. Lang

Fox
Chapel Publishing

CAMBIUM PRESS

This book is dedicated to my grandfather, James Lang, who sat me on his knee to show me how a micrometer worked; to my uncle, Archie lang, who couldn't resist sticking his finger in wet varnish on boat transoms, and to my son, Hunter Lang, who always wants to know the reason why.

—Robert W. Lang

Shop Drawings for Greene & Greene Furniture

© 2006 by Robert W. Lang

ISBN-13: 978–1–892836–29–8
ISBN-10: 1–892836–29–7

First printing: September 2006

A Cambium Press Title
John Kelsey, Editor

Cambium Press books are published by
Fox Chapel Publishing
1970 Broad Street
East Petersburg, PA 17520
www.FoxChapelPublishing.com

Library of Congress Cataloging-in-Publication Data

Lang, Robert W., 1953-
    Shop drawings for Greene & Greene furniture : 23 American Arts & Crafts masterpieces /
measured and drawn by Robert W. Lang
        p. cm
      ISBN 1-892836-29-7
1. Furniture -- Drawings. 2. Measured drawing. 3. Greene & Greene. 4. Arts and Crafts movement.
I. Title. II. Title: Shop drawings for Greene & Freene furniture.

TT196.L358 2006
684.1'04--dc22

                                        2006018908

                              Printed in China
                          10 9 8 7 6 5 4 3 2 1

Your safety is your responsibility. Neither the author nor the publisher assume any responsibility for any injuries suffered or for damages or other losses incurred that may result from material presented in this publication.

CONTENTS

INTRODUCTION

I was urged to write this book even before the publication of my first book, *Shop Drawings for Craftsman Furniture*. At the time I dismissed the idea, reasoning that the wonderful furniture produced by John and Peter Hall from the designs of Charles and Henry Greene was too detailed, too complex, and had too many subtle elements that couldn't possibly be shown in drawings. I still think that's a pretty good argument as I put the finishing touches on this work.

What caused me to go ahead was the realization that any book of drawings, or any woodworking text, can't possibly replace the actual experience of seeing fine furniture in the flesh, or the work and practice required to learn how to build it. At best, it can be a guide similar to a map that shows where a hiking trail goes up a mountain. The map can help you prepare, but it can't give you the experience of huffing and puffing up the final approach to the summit. It can't reproduce the smell of flowers or the sound of a waterfall along the way, but it can show you the shortest route, and it might keep you from walking off the edge of a cliff.

Accepting the limitations of what drawings can show, I fully realize that these drawings are only maps. If you want to build reproductions of Greene and Greene furniture, I sincerely hope that this won't be your only resource. Take the hike, climb the mountain, smell the flowers along the way and dip your feet in the waterfall.

But, these drawings are maps of a landscape that is rapidly eroding and that is the other reason I've embarked on this task. The designs created by the Greene brothers are becoming victims of their own popularity, confused by imitations that seek to capture the heart and soul by presenting the odd detail as the essence.

In later portions of this text I'll attempt to describe the elements of this furniture that can't be shown in mechanical drawings, but that again is only a substitute. There is also a list of useful books and information available online, but these too will not replace seeing the actual pieces. If you are truly interested in this furniture, a visit to any museum that has an original piece is well worth it, and a visit to Pasadena to tour the Gamble house and the Huntington collection might well be the pilgrimage of a lifetime.

My motivation for producing this book relates to my feelings about history, and the abundance of misleading published material and reproduction furniture that is labeled Greene and Greene but falls well short of the original pieces. Magazine articles promote the slapping of cloud lift details on improbable furniture forms and calling it Greene and Greene. Other articles push and pull perfectly proportioned original pieces into distorted forms to fit unlikely rooms and call the result a Greene and Greene reproduction, or present techniques as authentic that have never appeared in the original work. Furniture manufacturers are presenting collections labeled Greene and Greene and bearing the names of important Greene and Greene houses that are at best poor imitations of magnificent furniture.

I have no argument with any of this work itself, it's the presentation of these things as original examples that upsets me. The original work of Charles and Henry Greene holds a tremendously important place in the history of American design. As more people become aware of this work, they deserve the real thing. To learn from our history, we need to preserve as much information as we can, and be careful to distinguish adaptations from masterpieces. If we pass down to our children diluted examples, their children will say, "What's so special about that?" and this wonderful original work will be forgotten.

The legacy of Charles and Henry Greene was very nearly lost. A few individuals managed to save what remained and reawaken an understanding of the importance of their work. We all owe these people a debt of gratitude. We should also be grateful to those outside the realm of museums and other public institutions who have invested their money and time in preservation and understanding.

Along with this reawakening however, there have been some shameful incidents driven by greed, and the treatment of treasures as commodities. For every piece of Greene and Greene furniture that has come on the market under dubious circumstances, there has been a museum or collector willing to pay the price to become the owner. This attitude of owner rather than caretaker feeds the market and encourages more unscrupulous behavior. What purpose does it serve for museums to buy these pieces and then lock them away in the basement or deny access to those who would like to make a serious study of the details?

This could have been a more complete book if those people fortunate enough to be in possession of original works had given more than token cooperation. I'm grateful for the access I was given in my research, but I simply don't understand the reasoning that says sharing the details of this furniture isn't a benefit to the cause of preserving it. I don't think helping woodworkers understand how it is put together can be considered harmful.

I have always tried in my writing to do the work that was different, to approach my subject matter in a way that would fill in the missing pieces left by other works on the subject. There are a lot of books with Greene and Greene as part of the title, but few with much reliable information. This problem isn't limited to the subject at hand, but is common in the area of the history of woodworking and furniture construction. My hope is that this work will help to fill in some of the holes in the general understanding of the work of Charles and Henry Greene, and lead to a better appreciation of the significance of their original work.

My previous books have been solo efforts. I've done the research and made the drawings without any outside assistance. This time, however, there is a long list of people to thank, most importantly those woodworkers with more experience and knowledge in the subject who were so willing to share with me what they knew. This work would not have been possible without their contributions. The Yahoo! discussion group founded by Darrell Peart was especially helpful as I posed obsessive questions and rambled on with my theories. I'd also like to thank Christopher Schwarz of Popular Woodworking magazine for his patience and his willingness to ponder the methods and motives of woodworkers one hundred years ago. Dale Barnard deserves special praise for coming forward with information that only he could share.

Last mentioned but first on the list are my wife and son. Without their patience and support, and most importantly the love we share, none of this would be possible, nor would it matter.

Robert W. Lang
Maineville, Ohio, May 2006

THE BROTHERS

When Charles and Henry Greene opened their architectural practice in Pasadena, California, in 1894, they were part of a new breed of American architects, among the first to be formally educated within the United States. They had completed the two-year course in Architecture at MIT (then known as Boston Tech) in 1891 and each had worked for other architects in Boston before heading west.

At this time, many professions, such as law and medicine were going through the same transition in education, moving from apprentice-type training to a more formal education. As the country entered the modern age, things were changing, and more changes were on the way. In step with the times, the brothers were moderately successful in their first few years of practice, and each married shortly after the turn of the century.

Born in Cincinnati, they attended high school in St. Louis, and had the benefit of a unique high school curriculum. They attended the Manual Training School, which included courses in drawing, wood-work, and metalwork along with general studies. The inclusion of the manual courses wasn't intended to be for vocational purposes, but was meant to provide a sense of practicality and real-world skills. This had a beneficial effect on their later practice: both of them had an understanding of the materials and methods of putting things together to build a house.

Henry was skilled in practical engineering matters, and Charles was a woodworker and carver for all of his life. This enabled them to communicate directly and effectively with the craftsmen who fabricated their designs. Craftsmen have a lot more respect for a designer they know understands the work, and this enables the architect to learn from and make the most of available skills.

Their early houses were adaptations of historic designs, and as the 19th century ended, the influence of the Arts & Crafts movement became apparent. In 1901, the practice was successful enough for Charles to take an extended honeymoon in England, leaving Henry to take care of business back in California.

There is a tendency to portray Charles as the artistic dreamer, the brother with all the talent, and Henry as the practical business-man, the one who made sure the work was completed. While they had these tendencies, it is an oversimplification to put them in these neat little boxes. Like two sides of the same coin, they shared the same internal stuff, but the faces they presented to the world appeared different.

Most importantly, they functioned as a team, and neither would likely have been as successful without the other. Charles' focus on the artistic, and Henry's on the practical were choices they made, not reflections of innate abilities. The designs that have been identified as Henry's are just as creative and imaginative as those produced by Charles, and there is no evidence that Charles was inept in business or management.

In 1903 and 1904, things fell into place for the Greenes, and they soon found themselves extraordinarily busy. Clients were referring their friends and relatives, and in 1906, their work was featured in Good Housekeeping magazine. This wasn't just an increase in the volume of work, but an increase in the scope and type of work. In

1903, Henry moved the office to Los Angeles, and Charles began to work out of his studio at home. Their home designs began to include furniture pieces, which at this point were still derivations of Craftsman design. In 1905, they planned the Robinson house, the first house where they were given control of not only the house design, but also of the interior and furnishings.

There was also a great leap forward at this time in the designs of the furniture, and looking at the drawings for the Robinson house it appears as if this leap took place during the design phase. Some of the Robinson pieces are in their earlier style, but others, notably the dining room furniture, show the beginnings of the distinctive Greene and Greene design vocabulary.

In that same year, they planned the last of the Bolton houses and entered the most productive and creative years of their careers. By 1907, they had fifteen draftsmen on their payroll, working on the plans for the Blacker and Freeman Ford homes among others. These were followed by the Gamble, Pratt, and Thorsen houses. All of these homes were on a grand scale, costing 10 to 20 times the price of an average home of the day.

Building tends to be a boom or bust profession, and these few years are remarkable for both the quantity and the quality of work produced. There is a sense of joy and exhilaration in these designs, a celebration of the freedom to be creative and the pleasure of working at the peak of performance. The Greenes had successfully blended Arts & Crafts form with Oriental design to create their own unique style.

Rather than repeat their successful designs, the brothers grew and developed them. Each of the ultimate bungalow houses and the furniture designed for them builds on the previous work. Comparing these designs is like watching a child learn to swim or ride a bicycle. Once the basic skills have been mastered, there is a period of seeing how fast and how far one can go. There is a very real sense in the Greenes' work of joyous experimentation, taking concepts and expressions to their limits.

Henry Greene

By the spring of 1909, Charles Greene was in need of a break. The ultimate bungalows had been designed, several of them were completed, and the rest were either underway or ready to start. Charles and his family took an extended trip to England, returning in the fall. In the preceding four years, he had produced an amazing body of work, down to the smallest detail. Certainly, he had help from Henry and assistance from his draftsmen, but no one would be capable of keeping up that creative pace forever.

Charles Greene

When Charles returned, there was a change in the style of work. It isn't clear if this was by his choice, or if it was a result of economic constraints or the desires of clients. The excellence and attention to detail remained, but the work took a turn to a more formal, traditional style. 1910 was a slow year for the firm and when business picked up again in 1911 it was clear that the ultimate bungalow period was coming to a close. There would be additional furniture in the style for the Pratt and Gamble houses, but the home designs of this time, notably the Fleishacker and Culbertson houses, had an entirely different feel.

This change of pace doesn't mean that the

careers of the Greenes were over. Both brothers remained active for many years, but in different roles. Henry had not only managed the office while Charles was abroad, he also produced designs entirely of his own hand. The success of those years had been rewarding enough that they didn't need to keep up that pace. They had ensured themselves a comfortable life and made some adjustments personally and professionally. Some writers portray this period as forced retirement, two creative men growing old as the world turns away from their work and ignores them.

I think that Charles and Henry were as busy as they wanted to be after World War I. They had enjoyed tremendous success in the years before the war, and were resourceful enough to adapt to changing times if that had been their desire. That success gave them the freedom to ease up, to live and work to please themselves. After being partners for so many years, they each chose a different course.

Charles had always had desire to be an artist and an interest in eastern spirituality. In 1916 he moved his family north to Carmel. Working mainly by himself, his later work notably includes the Fleishacker house, and the James house. He also took a hands-on approach in his later years, personally creating carvings and furniture.

Henry remained in Pasadena, and settled into the role of local architect. He scaled back the size of the firm as the years went on, but continued designing new work and supervised the maintenance of their masterpieces.

THE OTHER BROTHERS

With all the talent that Charles and Henry Greene possessed, their work would not have been the same had it not been for the contributions of another pair of brothers, Peter and John Hall. Peter was the general contractor for most of the Ultimate Bungalows, while John ran the millwork shop, supervising the construction of the interior building elements as well as of the furniture.

There is an exponential advance in the quality of the work that occurred when the Halls became involved. It seems as if the pairs of brothers challenged and learned from each other. It's easy to imagine the Greenes thinking, "Let's see them build this," and the Halls thinking, "Let's see them design something we can't build." The synergy of this relationship produced some of the most incredible furniture ever made.

The furniture produced before the Halls was nice enough, but it lacked the special qualities of the later work. Clearly, the Halls and Greenes spoke the same language, and the skill of the Halls enabled the Greenes to take their designs to a new level, not limited by craftsmen unable or unwilling to produce work at that level.

Peter and John Hall were born in Sweden and moved to the United States before they were ten years old. Their father was likely a carpenter. Peter came to Pasadena in 1886 and spent the years between 1889 and 1892 in Seattle and Port Townsend Washington before returning. He was considered a master carpenter, notably a stair builder. In the world of finish carpenters, the man trusted with building the stairs is the most skilled man on the jobsite. The stairway is where all the skills of planning,

laying out, fitting and finishing must be performed at the highest level. The stairway is the most complicated part of the interior, and with its central location, it is often the showpiece of the interior.

Randall Makinson, in *Greene & Greene: Furniture & Related Designs*, asserts that Peter "had no formal training as a carpenter," but this makes little sense. Peter Hall was considered a master of his trade while still in his 20s, and this isn't a skill that someone just picks up one day. He may not have attended a trade school, but at the time, no carpenter would have. Training would have been an apprenticeship, starting in the early teenage years, perhaps under the tutelage of his father.

During the 1890s Peter worked as a carpenter, and in 1897 was listed as a benchman at the Pasadena Manufacturing Company, a local millwork shop. Brother John was equally skilled, and worked with his brother both on jobsites and at Pasadena Manufacturing. In 1897, John was listed as a carpenter for that firm. It isn't clear what is the distinction between these two positions, but it is likely that John had some seniority with the company over Peter.

In 1899, John was the foreman, where he remained until early 1907. In 1900, Peter left Pasadena Manufacturing and began to work as a general contractor. His first work for the Greene brothers was in 1904, and in July of 1906, he took out a permit to erect a carpentry shop, presumably to produce the millwork for the Robinson house for the Greenes.

In early 1907, the drawings for the furniture for the Robinson House were com-

John Hall

plete, as were the drawings for the Bolton House furniture. The shop was expanded, and John began working with brother Peter, running the shop and being directly responsible for building the furniture.

The shop wasn't very large, about 5,000 square feet, but it was well equipped with machinery driven by a line shaft and powered by a gasoline engine. A tremendous amount of work was completed in a relatively short period of time, so the shop must have been run efficiently and expertly. And this was not the type of work that could be rushed through the mill. The expressed joinery and intricate detail of the furniture is also present in the trim and built-ins. This work was produced by highly skilled men, working at a very efficient pace.

The interior of the Blacker house, for example, was completed in just five months and is almost entirely of wood. The Gamble house has the same amount of detail, and it was completed following the work for Blacker. Furniture production and millwork were produced in the same shop in the same relative time frame, but the completion of the furniture for any particular job was as much as a year behind the completion of the house.

There was some overlap in the furniture construction. A letter to Charles Green from Peter Hall in 1909 discusses both the Blacker and Gamble furniture nearing completion. In addition to being extremely busy, the Halls' shop was also likely crowded. The only known photos of the inside of the shop are mostly pictures of completed furniture, taken against a lumber rack or in front of a draped cloth. The only picture showing the equipment in the shop was taken in the 1920s, when the Halls manufactured small decorative boxes for fruit and candy.

The early 1900s were a period of transition in the woodworking industry, and cabinetmakers of the day were beneficiaries of this transition. Most of the stationary machinery in use today, table saws, band saws, planers, joiners, mortisers, and shapers existed and had been in common use for years. But handtool skills had yet to fall out of use. These men had access to the best of both the machine and handtool worlds, and they were likely the most adept woodworkers of all time.

Free of the grunt work that the machines could perform, they had the skills and the tools to perform by hand the details that were better produced that way. The furniture of Greene and Greene shows an interesting combination of both hand and machine techniques. The ever-present expressed joinery could be cut by machine - box joints and drawer joints on the table saw, and then the exposed edges lovingly refined by hand work. One of the challenges to making successful reproductions of this work is in knowing which method to use when.

After the peak years, Charles Greene commissioned some pieces personally in 1913. It isn't clear if these were all for his own use, or if he was seeking to develop a line of manufactured furniture. He copyrighted an intricate shop mark, and displayed a rosewood writing desk in the window of a local store. As work for the Greenes slowed to a standstill, the Halls switched to the production of redwood boxes until the shop was destroyed by a fire in the early 1920s. After the fire, Peter Hall returned to general contracting, and was busy building houses until his death in 1939. John continued to work in the area, sometimes for his brother, and sometimes for the Greenes.

During the peak years, John Hall's role as foreman was critical to the success and to the flow of work through the shop. It would have been his responsibility to review the architectural drawings, develop plans for the actual construction of the furniture, and direct the cabinetmakers. While there are numerous architectural drawings of the furniture in existence, there aren't any shop drawings prepared for actual construction. This is usually attributed to the fire that leveled the shop, but I don't think that formal drawings were ever prepared by the Halls.

The practice of creating shop drawings is relatively recent. In practice, architectural drawings don't show construction details, only the intent of the architect for the finished appearance. The drawings that exist today appear to be presentation drawings for the clients, examples of what to expect in the finished work. In most cases, there is some significant change from these drawings to the finished work. In today's litigious world, most millwork shops create their own drawings as a defensive measure. Architects also like to see shop drawings, to ensure that the work will be up to their standards. The gap between the two parties is much greater today than it was between the Greenes and the Halls.

Some of the drawings have penciled notes or sketches, but rarely are significant details shown. Where details do appear, they are in drawings prepared in later years. I see this as explaining to someone other than the Halls how the Halls would have made the details. Charles Greene made it a habit to stop by the shop on a daily basis. These visits are usually explained as his checking and directing the work, and this was certainly part of the reason.

Stories of Charles directing the carvers as their work progressed, to integrate his designs with the flow of the figure of the wood, make sense as this shows in the finished work. Stories of him picking up tools and working alongside the craftsmen are likely romantic nonsense the man would have been too busy for that. The main reason for Charles' visits to the shop was to work out construction and design details with John Hall. In all likelihood, each day's or week's work, and each new set of drawings, would produce a list of questions about how to proceed on the next step. With a good working relationship, and a common language, Charles and John would have been able to resolve these questions with a quick conversation and perhaps a quick sketch.

Peter Hall

One thing that is clear about the production of this work is that time wasn't wasted. Once the design vocabulary for a particular project had been established, it wouldn't make sense for every detail of every piece to be drawn, then sent back and forth from the shop to the office for approval and correction. John Hall would have prepared story poles from the drawings, checked the details with Charles when he came in the following morning, and then proceeded to complete the work. Since these were all one-of-kind pieces, the story poles would end up in the scrap pile, there wouldn't be a reason to preserve them.

Some payroll and other records still exist, but there isn't enough information to determine exactly how many men worked in the shop, or who was responsible for what tasks. Given the amount of available space, between five and ten men would have had room to work. Some of the routine work, such as the preparation of veneered panels, may have been subcontracted, but a few skilled men produced a great deal of work in a limited amount of space.

The inlay work was especially time consuming. In many pieces, there were as many or more hours in the inlay as there was in the construction of the piece that contained it. There probably was a bench in the corner of the shop where one man created this intricate work. The sequencing of other work would have been affected by this bottleneck, and this is mentioned in the Peter Hall letter of 1909. Some of the Blacker furniture is mentioned as being nearly ready, but waiting for the inlays to be completed so that it can be finished.

One of the reasons for the efficiency of the shop was the presence of up to date machinery, and the way that it was used. The drawer joints, discussed on page 35, are one example of machine-made joints in pieces with many hand-worked details. The machines that didn't exist in the day, hand-held routers and power sanders, are what many woodworkers of today depend upon for treating edges and smoothing surfaces. The use of these machines today is what can take the subtlety and liveliness out of reproductions of this furniture.

Flat surfaces would have been prepared by smoothing plane and scraper, joints adjusted to a perfect fit with shoulder planes, and numerous details were created by hand carving. The rounded corners that are so common were formed with a block plane and a spokeshave. All of these surface and finish details are finely done in the originals, and there is a good deal of variation that isn't possible unless this work is done by hand.

The rounded edges in particular have a great deal of personality due to being shaped by hand. Where an electric router will form a consistent radius along an edge, the rounded edges in Greene and Greene furniture shrink and grow in relation to other parts of the furniture, and to where the edge is located. The corners of breadboard ends for example, are much rounder and softer than the rest of the edges. This soft corner makes the furniture appear more organic and animated.

In addition to the handwork on surfaces and edges, there are some other interesting quirks in the construction methods used in the Hall's workshop. The Halls and their men were adept with hand tools, and obviously enthusiastic about the use of machinery. They also were absolutely committed to making the finest product possible, and this commitment led to some methods that are seldom, if ever, employed in most furniture.

Mortise-and-tenon joinery was common at the time, and has been a primary furniture joint for hundreds of years. Pegs securing the two pieces of the joint are not unusual, especially in the Arts & Crafts period. The square pillowed shape of the plugs used in Greene and Greene furniture take a lot more effort than other methods. Certainly a system was developed that allowed this work to be done expeditiously, but this is a very labor intensive detail. The plugs aren't the only extra step taken in the typical mortise-and-tenon joint.

As seen in X-rays of some pieces taken by the Los Angeles County Museum of Art, tenons are typically housed. In addition to the deep mortise to receive the tenon, a smaller mortise was cut about 1/8 inch deep around the edges of the main mortise. This allowed the edges of the shoulder of the adjoining piece to be hidden. In addition to making a strong enough joint incredibly strong, this method ensures that the perpendicular line of the joint won't ever show a gap, even if there is significant shrinkage in the piece containing the mortise.

This isn't a lot of material to remove, but it considerably raises the level of workmanship required to lay out and cut the joints. A typical single mortise must fit well, but there is some margin of error, and minor flaws and miss-cuts will be hidden in the finished joint. In the housed joint, the piece itself becomes a tenon, and the secondary mortise has to be precisely located and carefully sized. This also creates a complication for the edges of the two pieces, for the edge can no longer be worked to the end of a rail before assembly.

The edges at the intersection must be carefully shaped with sharp tools and sharp hand-and-eye coordination. Once the joint is together, there isn't room to get into the corner with a plane or spokeshave. The edges must be shaped with a chisel or knife, working into an already smoothed surface. In addition to being highly skilled, these workers also had to be confident and courageous to adopt this as a standard joint.

Where two horizontal pieces meet in a common vertical piece, the mortise and tenon locations are offset, rather than shortened. The length of the tenon is the critical element to the strength of this joint, and this is another instance where the quality of the finished work was put before the amount of labor expended. This adds time to every step of the layout and set-up work. It also increases the risk of ruining a part by cutting it the wrong way. In most cases, this can be seen by the arrangement of the plugs that secure the joints. The variation in layout isn't only decorative, it is an accommodation to these careful joints.

The LACMA X-rays also reveal the use of screws as fasteners, hidden below the ebony plugs. This is sometimes interpreted as a shortcut, but the reliance on the use of fasteners was more of an insurance policy than an expedient. In most cases, there were alternatives to screws and plugs that would have been faster, though not as secure. Screws were also used to fasten caps to the top of drawer sides and fronts. These appear to be brass pins at first glance, for the screw heads have been filed down below the level of the slots. Men who would file down the heads of a dozen brass screws in a single drawer were not the kind of men who were out to take shortcuts.

Another detail that is overbuilt is the hanging of doors. In a typical cabinet door from the outside it appears to be a single continuous hinge, similar to a piano hinge, but with a thicker barrel. Opening the door reveals a stack of butt hinges, with the last hinge carefully cut and filed to the exact length of the door stile. Apparently, the strength of a piano hinge was desired, but the available hardware wasn't good enough. The hinges used were of the highest quality. Similar hinges are still available, but cost eight to ten dollars each. To stack six or seven hinges together would raise the hardware cost as well as greatly increase the labor required.

The source of these details can't be determined. We don't know if the Greene brothers insisted on these methods, or if they came about at the suggestion of the Halls. The Greenes were more knowledgeable than most architects due to their early training and interest in woodworking. The Halls understood what the Greenes wanted and expected, and likely had a significant amount of input. If time travel ever becomes available, I'd like to go to Pasadena in 1908 or 1909.

THE TOWN AND THE CLIENTS

Today Pasadena sits on the edge of greater Los Angeles, where the suburbs and freeways meet the mountains, the boundary between the city and the raw beauty that is native California. In the early 1900s, Los Angeles wasn't much of a town, San Francisco was the center of West Coast civilization, and Pasadena was out in the country among the orange groves.

At the turn of the 20th century, Pasadena was becoming a resort, a destination for the wealthy from back east to spend the winter. Anyone who has been through a winter in Michigan or Ontario can appreciate the appeal of sunny skies and warm weather in the middle of January. There isn't any bad time to be wealthy, but one-hundred years ago was an excellent time. Income taxes didn't exist, and the fruits of the industrialization of America and the rapid growth that came with it were plentiful.

Many resort areas came into being around this time, places for the well-to- do to escape. One of the reasons for the need to escape is that the large cities of the East and Midwest weren't just crowded and ugly, they also posed some serious risks to health. Tuberculosis didn't have a cure, and the coal fires that powered the factories and mills and provided heat made cities miserable places full of soot and smoke.

In the summertime, the Adirondack Mountains of upstate New York, and the beaches along the Atlantic, were the places to go. Private trains brought the wealthy to beautiful homes called camps and cottages. In the wintertime, the logical place was California for its mild, and perhaps more important, arid climate. Florida was still mostly swamp at the turn of the last century, and a visit there came with the risk of malaria or typhoid fever.

Entrepreneurs in Pasadena built hotels that catered to these winter guests, and developers created neighborhoods where they could build their own vacation or retirement homes. Several of the Greenes' clients first came to California for a winter vacation, often staying for months at a time. The allure of climate and setting became so strong that it seemed only natural that many of them would stay.

In 1893, two young architects with degrees from MIT and apprenticeships with well-known Boston firms arrived to visit their parents who had moved west for health reasons. Their visit became relocation, and their eventual success came as a result of being in the right place at the right time, and of getting to know the right group of people.

Today we would call it networking, and Charles and Henry turned membership in a social club and good word of mouth from a few wealthy clients into successful careers. In the fall of 1895, the brothers joined the Twilight Club, a place to hear concerts and lectures as well as to gather socially. In time, more than a dozen club members would become their clients.

In 1901, Charles purchased land in the Park Place neighborhood, overlooking a canyon that today is the site of the Rose Bowl. Within a few years, the adjacent lots would become the setting for several Greene and Greene designed homes. Many of their clients came as referrals from other clients. Jenny Reeve was the mother of Mary Darling and a good friend of Adelaide Tichenor. Mrs.

Tichenor was from Ohio, and the widow of a lumberman.

Wealth from the lumber business was another common thread among the clients of Greene and Greene. Henry Robinson speculated in lumber and mining, and Robert Blacker and William Thorsen had made their fortunes in the lumber business. Thorsen had married the daughter of his boss, who was Blacker's sister-in-law. Caroline Canfield Thorsen had attended Vassar with Mary Pratt, whose husband Charles was one of the founders of Standard Oil and an owner of a California hotel.

Business and family connections accounted for most of the large commissions during the busy period between 1905 and 1910. Henry Robinson had been mentored by David Tod Ford, the president of Youngstown Iron and Steel. The Greene's were renovating a house for Ford, and were asked to build a house next door for Robinson. Ford's son Freeman Ford was vice-president of the Pasadena Ice Company, and would later commission the Greenes for a house of his own.

James Culbertson, another Michigan lumber investor, commissioned a house in 1902, and his three sisters built a house in 1911. There were also loyal clients such as Dr. William Bolton, who had three separate homes built by the Greenes between 1900 and 1906. Bolton died before the last house was completed, and his widow rented the house to Belle Barlow Bush. After commissioning furniture for her home, Bush moved back east in 1914, and the Culbertson sisters purchased the house.

Without their talents and business acumen, these connections wouldn't have been possible, and the pool of clients that could afford to build a Greene and Greene home was understandably small. For a few years

Charles and Henry had more work than they could handle, clients that were willing to turn them loose and provide a complete home from landscaping to furnishings.

In 1912, things began to change, not just in Pasadena, but also in the entire country and in the world of art and architecture. With the advent of World War I the economy slowed, and tastes and attitudes began to change. The willingness to experiment of the Arts and Crafts movement was replaced with a desire to return to a largely imagined past with the Colonial Revival movement.

After the war, the wealthy weren't quite so wealthy, and the spirit of excellence of Arts and Crafts was replaced with the sterility and coldness of the Modern movement in architecture. The Ultimate Bungalow period would end, but the brothers Greene would continue in creative work, although at a much slower pace and at a smaller scale.

THE FURNITURE

The furniture designed by Charles and Henry Greene, and built by Peter and John Hall, holds a special place in the history of American design. Built in the early years of the 20th century, it is in the context of the Arts & Crafts movement but rises to a level above and beyond any other furniture of the period. The majestic grace of the designs combined with the flawless craftsmanship of the construction makes it a favorite among all who value fine furniture and beautiful wood.

Unlike other examples of the period, this furniture was custom-made for specific places in the homes of very wealthy clients. The Greenes had much in common with other period designers such as Gustav Stickley, but where Stickley designed for mass production, Charles and Henry Greene designed pieces that were one of a kind. The best examples of their work were made without real regard to cost, and were lavished with an attention to detail that is rarely seen except in furniture made for royalty.

Most people have only seen photographs of this furniture. Only around 400 pieces were made, and most of them are now museum pieces or in the hands of private collectors concentrated in southern California. As visually stunning as photographs can be, seeing this work in person raises the level of experience to a much higher degree. Like all sensual experiences, there is a vast difference between the real thing and any depiction or description.

Taking the experience one more step, to see the furniture in the context of its original interior, instead of in a museum, can be breathtaking. Seeing the furniture in place also puts it, and the talents of the Greenes, in perspective. While an important element, the furniture is only part of overall design schemes that have no peers past or present.

In the houses known today as "Ultimate Bungalows" the Greenes enjoyed the kind of freedom that few architects ever experience. The opportunity to design and build a house down to the smallest detail is rare, and to execute it as well as they did is even rarer. The interiors are designed and finished as if they were the furniture, and to be in one of these homes is to step inside another world. The genius of the Greenes and the skills of those who worked for them carry throughout the entire building and beyond.

Floor plans, exterior details, landscaping, and even the placement of buildings are at a level beyond adequate description, and nearly beyond imagination. The work of the Greene brothers is powerful stuff, not just the product of one genius, but the synergistic product of two great designers, and two great mechanics. This took the results exponentially beyond what any one person could achieve.

While in California to research this book, I found it hard to stay focused on the furniture when in one of the original houses. Anywhere the eye might wander there is another incredible detail, often in wood, but also in glass, ceramic, metal, fabric, and stone. These details are so captivating that any and all of them are worthy of study. But my expertise and first love is the furniture, and the many enchanting details that set it apart.

In the early 1900s, Gustav Stickley was the most influential figure in the American Arts & Crafts movement. While his main business was manufacturing furniture, he and his employees also designed houses and interiors along with metal, ceramic and fabric items. The quality of life was seen as a unified blend of work, community and character, and the home and the objects within and around it were seen as a reflection of that quality. Stickley voiced his opinions, and those of many others, in the pages of his magazine, *The Craftsman*.

Charles and Henry Greene were fans of Stickley. Their early work clearly shows his influence, and they kept scrapbooks of clippings from *The Craftsman*. The admiration was mutual: Stickley published complimentary articles on the work of the Greene brothers. There isn't any surviving documentation of correspondence or meetings, but Charles made a stop at the Pan American Exposition in Buffalo in 1901 where Gustav debuted his new line of furniture, and Stickley traveled to California a few years later.

Stickley's Craftsman furniture was used in many of the Greene's early houses, and even later projects like the Gamble house had rooms furnished with Stickley. Philosophically the furniture springs from the same roots, and many of the details seen in Greene and Greene furniture can be seen as originating with Stickley and then taken to the nth degree.

The early furniture designed by the Greenes shows this relationship rather directly. The White sisters' tea table, one of the earliest known pieces, looks like a design exercise, a few twists and turns added to a basic Craftsman theme. As the Greenes developed, Asian influences appeared, in the cloud lifts in the panel rails and pulls on the Tichenor furniture. Simple cloud lifts were also used as cleats in doors in projects from the first few years of the 1900s.

As powerful as the influence of Stickley and the Arts & Crafts ideal was, the influence of Oriental design was equally important. A well-thumbed, marked up copy of Japanese Homes and Their Surroundings was owned by Charles, and he made a visit to the Louisiana exposition in 1904 to visit the Japanese pavilion at the suggestion of a client. The combination of these influences was the starting point for the Ultimate Bungalows, the vocabulary that was chosen to speak the language of building with passion.

Greene and Greene furniture departs from the Craftsman influence in several details, but remains true to it in the sense of proportion, expressed joinery, and the way it is integrated into a unified design. One of the biggest differences is the sense of softness through the use of flowing curves and subtly rounded edges. One observer of the period described it "like butter that has been squeezed through a tube." There was also the inclusion of purely decorative elements such as inlays of carved wood, precious metals, mother of pearl, and semiprecious stones.

The expressed joinery in Greene and Greene furniture appears in a creative, artistic way. Where Stickley used simple joints to make a decorative statement, the Greenes raised them to an art form, lavishing hand-worked details that almost turn the joints into sculpture. In most cases, the joinery was overdone, more than what was structurally necessary, but the softness and rounded edges keep the effect from being overwhelming. Exposed mortises and tenons, bridle joints, and box joints were secured with decorative pins, often arranged in a decorative pattern.

Rarely do two flat surfaces intersect in the same plane, a breadboard end will be both thicker and wider than the tabletop it is attached to. Rails set back from legs, doors and drawers set back from rails. In almost every piece, there are little details that break the surface, making their presence

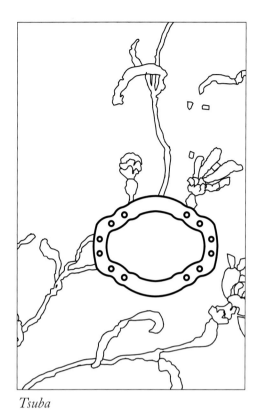

Tsuba

known to those who look close without shouting for attention.

Other elements are rendered in unexpected ways. Many table-tops extend far beyond the legs, giving the work an animated feel. In several tables with drawers, the fronts of the drawers extend several inches out from their frames, and chair arms twist and turn. The genius of the designs is that these elements never seem out of context. They fit in with the overall form of the piece, and with the design of the room.

Unlike a lot of Modern and Post-Modern furniture, these unusual elements aren't there just for the sake of being different. This is furniture that has been designed from the ground up. Nearly every standard element has been examined and rendered in a different form that meets the standards of structure and the desire for beauty. Most people who see Greene and Greene furniture for the first time don't say, "hmmm, that's different," they say "Wow."

One element that often appears is the tsuba, derived from the shape of Japanese sword guards. At the time, Japanese art was fashionable to collect, and tsubas were popular along with prints, watercolors, and pottery. The basic shape is derived from two intersecting ovals, and in Greene and Greene furniture it was used as an inlay pattern in a scale close to its actual size, and also on a grand scale, expanded to form the shape of a dining table. Parts of the shape will appear in nearby details, the bases of dining tables mimicking the intersecting curves of the top.

The other important Oriental element is the "cloud lift," reversing curves that form a step in long horizontal lines. In each house, these have a slightly different shape and form. In some cases, the lines aren't actually straight, but are very subtle arcs, and occasionally the lines leading into the lifts are not horizontal, but at a slight angle. The "typical" Greene and Greene cloud lift will only be typical to a particular house or room.

Many of the furniture details are like this, a continuing experiment in forms derived from a theme. In the few houses that have several rooms of furniture, each room has its own distinctive details. The inlay or carving in the dining room may be similar to that of the living room, but it will be a variation of the theme, not a reiteration. In all of the furniture there seems to be a willingness to experiment, a search for the ideal expression of the form.

Inlays appear in two distinct forms: carved wood floral forms that sit slightly proud of the background, and jewelry-like forms of metal, shell and stone. In some of the Gamble house inlays, the two forms are combined with carved wood branches leading to flowers of semi-precious stone.

Paneling, stairs, doors, windows, and all elements of interior trim are as nicely detailed and finely finished as the furniture. Built-in cabinets seem to have sprouted and grown from the surrounding woodwork, and the freestanding furniture feels like a permanent part of the designs. The concept of creating a cohesive environment is carried out from small elements like light switch plates and heating vents to massive exterior posts and beams.

Hard edges don't exist in these interiors, every change of direction is gently rounded, and the radius of these curves will vary slightly along the line. These transitions can be nearly imperceptible, but if you look at the corner of a tabletop, and then at the middle, you will see that the round over radius varies in size.

All of the wood used is of excellent quality, and the finishes are in a soft, satiny sheen. The many detailed elements are so subtly combined that it takes a while to take them all in and this is the essence of what makes this work so significant. In our era of short-cuts, we can look back at this example and explore what happens when no element is unimportant, no detail is insignificant, and there is no place for saying, "No one will ever see that, it's good enough."

There is a real sense of wonder in these creations, a sense of freedom like a wild horse running with the knowledge that there are no boundaries. For a brief period, Charles and Henry Greene had the opportunity to live in a world that most creative people can only dream of. There were clients with plenty of money and a willingness to see what the Greenes could do. There were craftsmen on hand who shared the vision and had the ability to make it a better reality. And most importantly, there was the creative drive behind it all, ready for this opportunity to excel.

WOODWORKING TECHNIQUES

This book assumes the reader has some experience with woodworking tools and joints, and is looking for techniques on the fine points of Greene & Greene furniture. Reproducing masterpieces isn't the easiest way to develop rudimentary skills. I would highly recommend taking a class and making some smaller, simpler, pieces for practice before tackling any of the pieces shown in the drawings of this book.

You can learn a lot from reading, but there isn't a good substitute for hands-on practice. If you can find someone knowledgeable to guide you through that practice, the learning curve will be much easier. One general woodworking book I highly recommend is *The Encyclopedia of Furnituremaking* by Ernest Joyce. There are also two good texts that were originally written in the early 1900s: *Modern Practical Joinery*, by George Ellis, and *The Complete Woodworker*, edited by Bernard E. Jones. I have found the period texts especially helpful in understanding the context in which the original Greene and Greene pieces were made. If you can put yourself in the shoes of the Hall brothers

and their employees, and understand the skills, tools, methods, and theories they worked with, your work will be much more successful.

My own training was based on the assumption that there are times when it makes sense to use a power tool, and other times when it makes sense to use a hand tool. Each has its place in my shop, and the decision to use one or the other is based on quality of the finished work followed by efficiency to produce the work. Like the Halls, I'm out to produce the best work that I possibly can, but I'm trying to make a living so I'm not going to fool around with inefficient techniques.

Developing the judgment to make these decisions about methods is to me a vital part of the training of a skilled cabinetmaker. As we look at the components of this furniture, I will include my opinions on how the work was originally performed, and how I would do it today.

In the early 1900s, most of the machinery we are familiar with today was available, and had been in common use for 20 or 30 years. Table saws, band saws, joiners, planers, shapers, and mortising machines were all available at the time, in forms that we would recognize. The Halls were adept at utilizing the efficiencies of their machinery, as is seen in their choice of drawer joints and their method of fabrication. These were modern men, using modern equipment and techniques.

What was missing in the woodshop of 1905 were the portable tools and abrasive equipment that are relied on so heavily today. The most significant tool missing from the Hall brothers arsenal is the

Greene and Greene furniture tends to be complicated. As you plan your work, think about subassemblies and the sequence for assembly.

portable router. All of the rounded edges we see in this furniture, and all of the carved and recessed details, were shaped by hand. While a plunge router will speed the making of mortises, going at the edges of these pieces with a roundover bit and calling it a day will result in sterile, lifeless pieces that won't quite look right. The same is true for carved details. It might be possible to jig up a router to make something similar, but if you're after the real thing, use the real tools and the real techniques. The most difficult and challenging aspect of this furniture is found in the small and subtle details.

Rounding edges

A low-angle block plane is the most effective tool to use for rounding edges. With the adjustable mouth open, and the iron set to take a relatively aggressive cut, knock the corner off a sharp edge and create a chamfer at roughly 45 degrees along the edge. Make the next cuts at progressively steeper and shallower angles, developing a faceted edge close to the desired radius. The beauty of the block plane, as opposed to the router, is that it is simple to vary the radius along the edge by taking a few more passes. The edge treatment on most Greene and Greene furniture has more of a radius at the ends and intersections of parts. Legs will be more rounded at the floor than at the tabletop, and the ends of tops will have the appearance of being worn as the curved edges meet at the corners.

After you have cut the edges roughly to size, adjust the mouth of the plane and the iron to take a shallow finishing cut. Plane off the obvious facets, then the areas in between, creating a smooth curved surface. This sounds like a lot of work, but with a little practice, it goes very quickly, leaving a surface that will only need a light sanding with a fine grit paper, if that. For rounding the edges of a curved surface, the block plane will work just as well on convex curves, but won't be effective on concave ones. For those areas, a spokeshave will work, using the same method of creating facets and then removing them.

For really tight curves, or at the end of a straight piece that terminates into another piece, you might need to use a chisel to shape the curve. I work as far as I can with the plane, then as far as I can with the spokeshave, leaving only a fraction of an inch to be formed with the chisel. A paring chisel or a carver's skew chisel then shapes this small remainder by hand. The alternative is to round the edges before assembly, which is simple enough unless there is a housed mortise-and-tenon joint on the end. In this case, if the mortise is radiused in the corner, the edge must match the radius of the mortise. If the housing is square, a relief cut is made first by placing the back of the paring chisel on the face of the piece containing the mortise, then, swinging the chisel to establish the curve. The edge can then be shaped by working into the relief cut.

Housed mortises

Authentic Greene and Greene mortises were housed. In addition to the mortise itself, an area surrounding the mortise the same size and shape as the piece containing the tenon is excavated to about $1/8$ inch. This serves two practical purposes: it makes the joint extremely strong, and it covers the shoulders of the tenon. If the piece containing the mortise should shrink away from the joint over time, the joint will not show a gap.

For this to look right, the secondary mortise, or housing, must be a snug fit around the edges of the tenoned piece. Obviously, this piece needs to be square and consistently sized if there is to be any hope of it looking good in the end. The gain in strength comes into play when the tenon is reduced in width, as when two rails meet at the same location on adjacent faces of a leg. I have drawn all of the joints in the drawings this way, but of course, the reader is free to use regular mortises and tenons.

In the Hall brothers' workshop, they likely used a mortising machine similar to today's hollow-chisel mortiser. Some machines of the era had a separate drill bit and chisel instead of an integrated configuration, but the principle is the same. In some pieces, like the Blacker house chairs, X-rays show that the mortises were chopped by hand. This was, I believe, the exception rather than the rule due to the location of the mortises and the curved shape of the rail containing them. It was faster to chop the mortise by hand than it would have been to set up the machinery to hold the curved part.

The two efficient ways to make mortises today are with either a hollow chisel mortising machine, or a plunge router. Mortises can also be made by removing the waste with a drill bit and cleaning up the joint with chisels, or by chopping them by hand with a mortising chisel. There is nothing wrong with any of these methods, but they will take considerably longer, and they take a good deal of skill to maintain accuracy in the size, shape and location of the mortises. If you choose one of these methods, doing the many mortises on any of these pieces will provide plenty of practice to develop your hand-tool skills.

Don't waste your time with a hollow-chisel attachment for a drill press. It sounds like a good idea, but there aren't any around that offer any degree of reliability or accuracy without an insane amount of fussing and fiddling. A dedicated hollow-chisel mortiser can be purchased for just a few hundred dollars, and if you're serious about building furniture it's a good investment in productivity.

I regularly use both a hollow chisel mortiser and a plunge router to cut mortises. There isn't an appreciable difference in time with either method, and they both have advantages and disadvantages. The router will leave a slightly cleaner hole, but the rounded ends of the hole will either need to be squared, or the ends of the tenons rounded or cut short to fit. If a project requires two different sized mortises, I will set one device up for one size, and the other tool for the other size.

The key in getting a hollow chisel mortiser to work properly is to ensure that all the elements of the machine are square to each other. The fence must be square to the base and parallel to the chisel, and the stroke of the chisel must be truly vertical in relation to the fence and the base. You may have to loosen or remove the column from the base to insert shims to align these parts. The time it takes to do this will be rewarded with parts that come together nicely. If you don't align the machine, you will be forever scratching your head wondering why every joint is just a little off.

The other improvement needed by most mortisers is a truly sharp chisel. I start by making sure the points on the end of the chisel are all the same length. With the chisel locked in the chuck without the drill bit, I place a sharpening stone or block of wood with #120 grit sandpaper attached on the base of the machine below the chisel. I bring the chisel down until the points begin to make contact with the stone. When they do, I move the stone back and forth while maintaining downward pressure to dress the points to the same length.

There will likely be one or two long points on the typical chisel, and this procedure will flatten them out. That's okay, because the next step will remedy that. If the points remain with slightly different lengths, the chisel will tend to lean as it is forced into the wood. This will cause sloppy joints, and burning, as the mortise is made.

The next step is to dress the inside of the chisel with a diamond cone sharpener. If the points are flattened or bent this will take a bit of work with a coarse cone. If the points are in good shape, it only takes a few moments of work with a fine cone to develop a wire edge on the outside faces of the chisel.

Most people stop at that point, or take a swipe or two on the outside to remove the wire edge. I prefer to dress and hone the outside faces in the same way I would flatten the back of a regular chisel rubbing over progressively finer stones to remove any irregularities in the faces. The argument against this is that it will decrease the size of the chisel, making the actual size of the mortise slightly less than the nominal size. This is a silly argument, because the tenon will be cut to fit the mortise, not to an exact dimension. The tenon won't know or care if the mortise is .368 inch instead of dead-on $^3/_8$ inch. The important thing is to cut the mortises quickly and neatly, and you need a sharp chisel for this whether you are doing it by hand or machine.

One of the disadvantages of the hollow chisel mortiser is that with most machines you need to layout every joint to determine the end points of the mortises. The most common mistake made in using these machines is to cut the joint the way you see it done on TV, from one end to the other, overlapping each progressive stroke. The proper way is to leave a space between each plunge of the bit, then to return and waste out the material remaining. If you try to cut a continuous slot, the chisel will bend in the direction of least resistance. This can lead to burning and damage to the bit and chisel. The chisel should always be surrounded by wood on all four sides or on two sides as it is plunged, not on three or one.

Routed mortises

When making mortises with a router, I recommend a three horsepower model with a decent fence. I work with a skinny guy who prefers a slightly smaller 2HP router, and unless you are in a production situation this will work fine. The best router bit to use is an up-cutting spiral bit. The less expensive high-speed steel bits work just as well as solid carbide, and aren't as likely to break or chip when you hit something hard.

Most woodworking books and magazines show jigs for cutting mortises with a plunge router that are far more complicated than they need to be, usually three sided boxes to contain the piece of wood and rails for the router to ride on. Stops to precisely locate the ends of the mortises are included, usually registering off the base of the router. The really fancy ones will use template guides and require the assistance of at least two engineers to build and use.

The fence of the router alone will locate the mortise in the width of the work, and it's entirely possible to stop and start the

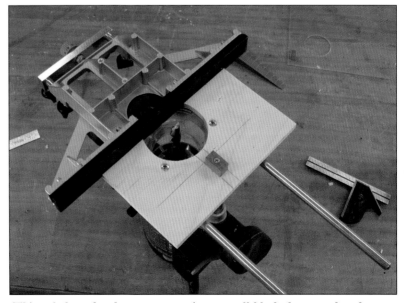

This sub-base for the router contains a small block that matches the diameter of the bit. Together with the fence, it will locate mortises with the aid of a notched template.

The leg and notched template are placed together in the bench vise. The block on the end of the template registers the template against the end of the leg.

This method allows mortises to be routed without the need for laying out and marking each and every joint.

mortises by cutting to a layout mark. What is crucial for a good mortise is that it is deep enough and that there is a good fit between the cheeks of the tenon and the walls of the mortise. The length doesn't really matter, and if you want to do any test fitting, the tenons should be a bit short so you can take the joint apart.

The main reason I see to use a jig to locate the mortises is to save time in laying out the work, and to alleviate the need to keep a close eye on the cutter. If I have just a few mortises to make, I'll lay them all out and stop the router manually. If there are many, then I will use the jig shown on page 25 and at left.

I've added an auxiliary base plate to the router that has a block of wood the same size as the diameter of the bit screwed to it, so that the edges of the block are in line with the edges of the bit. The template is quite simple: the notches represent the exact stop and start of each mortise. There is no need to allow for the distance from the edge of the router base to the edge of the bit, or for the offset of a template guide collar. The fence is set to locate the cutter the correct distance from the face of the work, the ends of the mortises are marked on the template in their actual locations in length, and the notches can be quickly cut. A small block is added to one end of the template to locate it a consistent distance from the end of the workpiece.

It the template is used on a wide enough piece to support the router, like a leg, the template and leg are clamped together in the bench vise. On narrower parts, like cabinet rails, I clamp the template to a group of identical parts. The group of parts supports the router, and when one set of mortises is cut, the stack is unclamped. The freshly mortised piece is moved to the back of the line, the template and clamps replaced, and the mortising can quickly continue.

Making housed mortises with this system is easy, provided that the thickness of the tenoned part matches the diameter of a router bit. After making the main mortises at $1/2$ inch or $3/8$ inch in width, replace the bit with one of a larger diameter that matches the thickness of the rail. Use the same template and guide block to locate the housings equally around the perimeter of the mortise.

If the main mortises are made with a hollow-chisel

mortiser, the housings become more complicated to make. I make them before cutting the deep mortise, knifing around the perimeter to establish the limits, then wasting out the interior with either a chisel or a router. There isn't much material to remove, the important thing is to get a nice clean line around the edges, and a consistent depth.

Tenons

There are also numerous ways to make tenons, ranging from cutting them entirely by hand to processes done with the table saw, band saw, or router table. The books mentioned earlier, by Ellis and Jones, both contained detailed descriptions of doing this with hand tools, and this can be relatively efficient if you have sharp, properly filed saws available. After the shoulder lines have been established, the remaining cuts are rip cuts. If you're serious about doing this by hand, you should have two decent saws.

I prefer to make tenons on the table saw, establishing the shoulders with the miter gauge or a sliding table, and then cutting the cheeks with a jig that holds the work piece vertically and runs along the rip fence. Again, it should be remembered that these are rip cuts, and the appropriate saw blade makes a lot of difference when making deep cuts. This jig is simple to make and is quicker to use than the commercially made jigs that ride in the miter slot.

Some woodworkers like to set up a dado stack in the table saw, and form the tenon cheeks with the workpiece flat on the table, guided by the miter gauge. If you use this method, you need to be very careful to keep the same downward pressure on the work with each pass. It's common to ease up a little with each succeeding pass, making a crooked or inconsistent tenon. A well, tuned band saw can also be used. I like to use it to form the ends of tenons and any haunches, after the cheeks have been cut with the table saw.

Whatever method is used to cut the tenons, they will likely need to be fine-tuned for a good fit. I aim to machine the tenons slightly oversized, then trim them to fit with a shoulder plane. With a cleat or stop attached to the surface of the bench, the tenons can be quickly fit without the need to clamp each one. Logic tells us that it should be possible to machine the tenons exactly, but experience finds that it is better to fit each one.

To ensure a good fit, machine the tenons slightly oversize and trim each one to fit. After fitting, mark the location on both parts.

A scrap of wood attached to the top of the bench acts as a stop so that the tenons can be trimmed without clamping them. A shoulder plane or a rasp will remove a small amount of material in a controlled manner.

Ebony plugs

With the mortise-and-tenon joints prepared and fit, the next detail to address is
the ebony plugs that appear to reinforce
the tenons. In many cases, they do, but in
some places, the plugs are only decorative.
The plugs are also used to cover the heads
of screws. Given the high price and brittle-
ness of ebony, and the time involved, I
think it makes sense to treat all of the
plugs in the same way, setting them in
holes $1/4$ inch to $3/8$ inch deep. This simpli-
fies fabricating the plugs, you don't have to
keep track of long ones and short ones, and
you don't have to whittle a long plug to fit
a hole through a mortise-and-tenon joint
of make a square hole all the way through
an assembled joint. Both of these methods
are often seen in published work, but are
incredibly time consuming. If you're considering either of these methods, count the
number of plugs in the piece you will be
building and reconsider.

I reinforce the mortise and tenon with a
round dowel, about an inch long. The
dowel, or any pin through the joint, doesn't
really make it any stronger, it only keeps the
joint from coming apart if the glue and
other elements of the joint fail. After making the square holes for the plugs, I drill
through the assembled joint with a brad
point bit, put glue on the dowel and drive it
in flush with the bottom of the plug recess.
There are different approaches to forming
these recesses, some of them reasonable and
efficient, and some of them a ridiculous
waste of time. Once again, you want to
count the number of plugs before you start.

You could use the hollow-chisel mortiser
to make the recesses, but you should adjust
the fit of the drill bit and chisel so that the
bit is higher up than it would be for cutting a full depth mortise. The bottom of
the hole will still be somewhat ragged, and
I think it's too tedious to locate the recesses exactly where they belong.

I prefer to locate the center of the recesses
and drill a round hole with a flat-bottom
forstner bit. If the plugs are in a regular
pattern, the layout work can be done on a
plywood template, and the centers of the
holes marked with an awl or punch. The
holes can then be drilled on the drill press
to keep them straight and of a consistent
depth. All that then remains is to square
up the holes.

This is another place where published
work shows some very slow and tedious
methods. Sometimes it looks like these
guys are paid by the hour instead of by
their results. If the holes have been established with the forstner bit, there isn't
much material to be removed to make the
recesses square, four light cuts with the
right-size chisel will do the job, but all of
the plug holes do need to be the same size,
and they won't look right if they aren't parallel or square. If there are just a few, this
method will work, and it is good practice,
but on a larger project you want a way to
cut all four sides at once, and to guarantee
that the size is correct.

I use a modified chisel from the hollow-
chisel mortising machine. At first glance,
this might seem like a wasteful use of the
tool, but it's less expensive than a good
quality chisel, and it makes quick work of
making perfect square recesses. Grind the
points down until there is just a bit of a
curve remaining between them, and then
hollow out the insides of the corners with a
Dremel tool. Hone the outside of the chisel until it is sharp and you're ready to go.

If the plugs are in a straight line, clamp a
piece of $3/4$ inch thick plywood tangent to
the line of round holes that were made
with the Forstner bit. This establishes one
edge of the recesses, and keeps the plugs in
a nice straight line. A few hammer blows
on the square chisel will establish the
recess - you can hear and feel when you've

reached the bottom of the drilled hole. I use a steel hammer, and the end of the chisel will eventually mushroom from this. If that makes you feel guilty, you can use a mallet, or make a wooden handle to fit over the shank of the chisel. I don't mind because with the points ground off, that chisel isn't going back in the mortising machine anyway. There may be a tiny sliver of wood remaining in the bottoms of the corners, but this can be quickly removed with a small paring chisel.

Not all Greene and Greene pieces have square plugs. In some early and late pieces, they are round, as in the Robinson dining room and in the Charles Greene sideboard. These round plugs protrude about $1/32$ inch and the edges are just barely broken, the exposed faces of the plugs being flat.

The square and rectangular plugs are best described as being pillowed. They are gently rounded on their faces, with a slight radius on the edges. These protrude $1/16$ inch or less, and the radius on the edge ends where the plug meets the surrounding wood. Making them pyramid shaped is a neat trick, but it isn't authentic, and trying to shape and finish the ends of the plugs after gluing them in place is a good definition of insanity. It's much easier to round the ends, cut them to a consistent length, and then put them in place.

If you can find and afford ebony, you can make the plugs from the same material as was used originally. Ebony is so hard that it is brittle, so you need to be careful with it. I prefer to use ebonized walnut, which is much less expensive and far easier to work. After discussing how to make and shape the plugs, we'll look at ways to make the walnut black. The fabrication techniques are the same for either wood, and other hardwoods can also be used so long the plug material is slightly harder than the surrounding wood.

The plug material should be milled just slightly larger than the recesses they will fit in. The exact size depends on the species used for each piece, but it will be on the order of a few thousandths of an inch. The idea is that the harder plug will compress the sides of the recess and a nice tight fit will be the result. It's a good idea to test the fit on some scrap before committing to a final size for the finished work. In theory, the final size can be achieved right from the saw, but it's

A plywood template is used to mark the centers of square plug locations. After marking, holes are drilled to a consistent depth with a Forstner bit.

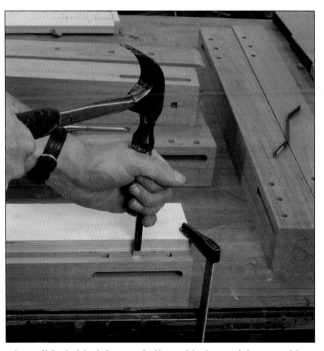

A modified chisel from a hollow chisel mortising machine makes the round holes square. A scrap of plywood clamped to the leg tangent to the holes registers one edge of the plugs and keeps them aligned.

A small flat riffler file cleans up the edges and bottoms of the square holes.

Making the plugs a consistent length, and pillowing the ends before inserting, speeds what can be a tedious process. Chamfer the back edges of the plugs and spread glue around the hole before tapping them in with a dead-blow hammer.

better to sneak up on it using a planer or a thicknessing sander.

There are several good methods for shaping the ends, and with any of them you want to leave the blanks for the plugs long enough that you can safely hold on to them. You don't want to stick the ends of your fingers into a sander because the pieces are too short. My preference is to cut the blanks between 1inch and $1^{1}/_{4}$ inches long, and shape the ends on a vibrating sander that has a stiff pad. What grit to start with again depends on the species, but #100 or #120 is reasonable. Sand through two or three progressively finer grits to achieve a polished surface on the ends.

You can also use self-adhesive sandpaper on a flat surface, or you could glue regular sandpaper down with contact cement, and twirl the ends on different grits by hand. With either method you need to practice on a few to get the desired look. With short pieces you can flip them end for end and get two polished ends at a time. Some people prefer to use a longer stick, shape and polish an end, cut a plug off, then repeat the process. I'd rather get a bunch of ends polished, then cut the entire batch to finished length, but the longer stick method is less wasteful of materials.

Cutting the plugs to length is straightforward, but because they are so short, it needs to be done safely. I wouldn't try to cut pieces this small with a table saw or a powered miter saw, they are too likely to be pulled into the blade. Cutting them by hand, with a bench hook or shop-made miter box with a stop won't be as tedious as you might think. The cutting to length can also be done on the bandsaw, using the miter gauge with a stop attached. There isn't much room between the blade and the stop on the miter gauge, so I use the point of my awl to hold the piece safely against the stop.

When all the plugs are cut to length, chamfer around the back edges with a chisel or knife to make it easier to start them in the holes. I put a little dab of glue around the inside edges of the hole, set the chamfered end in the hole, and drive the plug home with a dead-blow mallet.

Ebonizing

To ebonize, or turn the walnut black, I prepare a solution from white vinegar and steel wool. I use the cheapest white vinegar from the grocery store, put it in a plastic container, and shred a piece of #0000 steel wool into the liquid. In three or four days, enough of the iron in the steel wool will go into solution in the vinegar to cause a chemical reaction with the tannic acid in the walnut.

The container must be left uncovered. As the iron works into the vinegar, gas is formed and a closed container will explode. The liquid remains clear, and it should be strained through a paper coffee filter placed in a funnel before use. Brush the solution on the walnut, and it will turn black within a few minutes. The color change is caused by a chemical reaction, so it will penetrate below the surface of the wood. Let the parts dry thoroughly before placing them in the finished piece. If you try to color after assembly, the solution can react with or bleed into the surrounding wood.

Breadboard ends

Breadboard ends are used on horizontal panels, disguising the end grain and stiffening the top against possible warping or cupping. The Greenes and Halls were crazy about breadboard ends, and often used them at the end of fixed and adjustable shelves as well as tops. In most cases, there is a variation in thickness between the top and the breadboard, with the breadboard generally about $1/8$ inch thicker than the top. This difference is usually split evenly between the top and the bottom, but in some pieces, the breadboard is flush on the top and in others, it is flush on the bottom. The breadboard is also $1/8$ inch to $1/4$ inch longer than the width of the top.

The trick to making breadboard ends is to hold them firmly to the top, while allowing the top to expand and contract as the seasons change. A tongue worked across the end of the top fits in a groove along one edge of the breadboard. Both archive drawings and X-ray images have documented that the breadboards were attached with long screws driven in from the outer edges into the tongue, the screw heads hidden behind the ebony plugs. The holes through the breadboard near the ends are elongated to allow the screws to swivel as the wood in the top moves. Screws near the center go through a hole the size of the screw shank, fixing the center in place and equalizing the movement on either side.

At the front and back edges of the top, a proud spline is commonly seen, accenting the joint and covering the

Clamp a straight edge across the end of a top to act as a guide for a router to form the tongue for the breadboard end. A combination square will set the distance quickly and accurately.

A router with a straight edge on the base will track along the straight edge more accurately than a round base model. If tenons are included along with the tongue, leave some material at the edge of the top to support the router base while cutting the shoulder of the tongue.

Fine-tune the fit of the tongue, and refine the edge of the shoulder, witrh a shoulder plane.

If the breadboard end is thicker then the top, be sure to account for that when milling the grooves for the tongue and splines.

end of the groove in the breadboard. The splines don't stick out very far, usually $1/16$ inch to $1/8$ inch depending on the season. The groove for the splines is $1/2$ inch to $3/4$ inch deep.

In some pieces, the breadboard is further reinforced with a tenon extending from the tongue. This is the case when a plug is seen on the top of the breadboard as well as at the outer edge. As with the screws, tenons near the center can be a tight fit in the width of the mortise, but in the joints near the ends, some allowance should be made for movement of the top.

In the original pieces, the tongues and grooves were likely formed by machine methods. The tongue can be cut by clamping a straightedge across the top, and running a router equipped with a straight cutter along this guide. The top is then flipped over, and the cut is repeated, forming the tongue; $1/2$ inch is an adequate length for the tongue, but another $1/8$ inch or $1/4$ inch will make a stronger connection. If there are tenons in addition to the tongue, set up the router and edge guide so that the first cut makes a groove across the end of the top, establishing the shoulder of the joint. This leaves full, thickness material at the end of the top that will support the base of the router as the tenons are cut. It's possible to get a clean shoulder and the right size tongue directly from the router, but because the location is usually visible and the joint attracts attention, it's wise to be cautious and machine the tongue a little large, then fine-tune the thickness and shoulder with a plane. This is an excellent way to justify the purchase of a good shoulder plane.

Making the groove in the breadboard is straightforward if the tongue is made to match the size of an available cutter. The key is to get it properly located vertically so that the offset between the top and the breadboard end is correct. The groove for the spline can be tricky to cut because of the offset. You can make it in both pieces at once by using a slot cutter in a hand-held router, with the two pieces dry-assembled. Attach scraps of veneer or other material to the thinner top so that the router will be level while cutting the groove. The slot cutter will leave a ramp at the beginning and end of the groove, which can be cleaned out with a chisel.

Make the splines as rectangles, and carefully fit them to

the length and thickness of the groove. I mark the curved profile of the spline with a pencil, remove it from the slot and cut the outer edge on the bandsaw. After smoothing out the saw marks and rounding over the edges it is ready to be permanently attached. It's tempting to glue the spline in place and trim the outer edge with a router bit with an offset bearing, but I have never been brave enough to try it that way.

Assemble the breadboard end to the top to make certain that everything fits, and then take it apart to round the edges where the pieces of varying thickness meet and to finish-sand the top. The long edge of the breadboard, where it meets the top, demands special attention. It should have a slight radius that ends just a hair above the intersection. If you go too far it will show as a gap between the parts and if you try to sand the radius after assembly, it's too easy to put cross-grain scratches across the end of the top.

Cloud lift

The cloud lift is one of the signature features of Greene and Greene furniture, and those who haven't carefully studied these pieces assume there is a typical way to do it, that the same pattern was duplicated in different projects at different times. This is one of the subtleties that is difficult to show in drawings and harder to get right in real life. The cloud lift was a theme, not a repeated detail. Like many of the details, each house, and often each room in a house, had its own distinct variation.

To get the cloud lifts right, the lines and curves need to be the right size, in the right places, and symmetrical from one end to the other. The best way to make them is to work out a pattern in plywood, and when it looks right, cut a template from that pattern. Start by drawing two parallel lines, and connect them with a line drawn at an angle where the curves intersect. A 45-degree angle is a good place to start, but in some pieces it is 60 degrees and in others it is nearly vertical.

With a draftsman's circle template, start sketching in the curves that connect the three lines. The correct radii will be tangent to the parallel lines and leave a small portion of the angled line between the two curves. When the curves and lines look right, cut just outside the lines with a bandsaw, and smooth everything back to the lines with a rasp, a file, or sandpaper.

It's well worth the time invested in making a template for cloud lift patterns. Using the template will make parts that are identical and symmetrical. Before routing, trim the parts with a bandsaw or jigsaw, so that the router is removing only a minimal amount of material. I prefer using a small diameter bit with a bearing on the bottom. This lets me see what I'm doing, and will form a tighter inside curve.

Add a fence to locate the edge of the template to the rail and trim the end to locate it on the end of the work piece. Make sure the edges are square so you can flip it over to use on both ends.

Remove most of the waste with the bandsaw or a jigsaw, cutting as close as you can to the line while staying on the waste side of it. I use a flush trimming bit in a router to clean off the saw marks, but they could be cleaned up with a rasp, block plane or spokeshave. The router ensures symmetry and accuracy, but includes the risk of tearing out some of the material, especially where the curves reverse. Don't try to remove too much material at once and pay attention to the direction of the grain while routing.

Proud box joint

The proud box joints in the drawers of some pieces are made, in theory, the same way as a standard box joint with the fingers left long. Since this is a Greene and Greene detail, it's a bit more complicated. The usual way to cut a box joint is with a jig on the table saw that registers the space between the fingers and the width of the cutter. The problem here is that the fingers get progressively wider from top to bottom in the drawer. This eliminates the automatic spacing, but the cuts can still be made by passing the ends of the parts vertically over the saw blade or dado stack.

Make a sled that is at least as wide as the distance between the two miter slots on the saw table, attaching it to two runners that slide in the slots. Make a cut in the sled to locate the position of the blade in the base, and attach a fence to the back of the sled at a right angle to the saw kerf. Make the fence tall enough and sturdy enough that you can clamp the parts to it and keep your hands out of the path of the blade.

Set the height of the blade above the base of the sled the thickness of the adjacent part, plus the amount of offset in the finished drawer box. Lay out the joint and then make the cuts by clamping the parts to the sled, lining up the cut lines to the kerf in the base of the sled. Be sure to indicate in your layout which side of the line is waste and which side is kept. Carefully make each edge cut, and then make repeated cuts in between to remove the waste.

Don't expect to produce a finished joint in your first attempt. This is going to take some practice. The joints shouldn't be too tight, but there shouldn't be any visible gaps. You can make slight adjustments to the widths of the fingers with a rasp or file. When you have a good fit, take a sharp pencil, and mark around the edges where the parts intersect. These marks will serve as a guide in rounding the edges. This is best accomplished with the joint apart, working each edge round while leaving the pencil line.

Make the square recesses for the plugs with the joint apart, then put the two ends of the joint in place, barely starting one into the other. Brush glue sparingly on the surfaces of the joint, and bring the parts together. Instead of clamping, screw the pieces together, locating the screws at the locations of the plugs.

DRAWER MYSTERY

Rabetted tongue-and-groove drawer joint.

Of all the details in Greene & Greene furniture, the most intriguing to me are the drawer joints. I'm not fascinated because they are intricate or challenging to make. It's the mystery of the things, why were they made the way they were, and why, in one house, were they done differently?

Except for the proud box joints in some of the Gamble and Blacker house pieces, the Halls used a rabbeted tongue and groove joint as seen at right in almost all of their work. Some kitchen cabinet drawers had a simpler rabbet joint, but this one was used often enough to be considered "typical Greene and Greene."

For all the attention paid to other time-consuming details in rarely seen places, it seems out of character not to see dovetailed drawers. The dovetail joint is today, and was at the time, considered a hallmark of fine craftsmanship and of a well-made drawer. In woodworking textbooks of the period, other joints for drawers were not even discussed.

With the growth in the use of power tools and machinery since the early 1900s other joints, including the one used typically by the Halls, are seen in reference books, usually with the explanation that this is an easier, faster and less demanding joint to make. There is also an understanding that it isn't quite as good as a dovetail.

The furniture and built-ins at the Thorsen house are the only known example of dovetailed drawers in Greene & Greene furniture made by the Halls. The Thorsen house is something of a special case, being located in Berkeley, hundreds of miles away from the Pasadena shop. A crew of workers was sent to the jobsite, and the furniture and built-ins were made in a temporary shop set up in the basement "Jolly Room."

While this joint may have made an appearance in Scandinavian Modern furniture in the 1920s and 1930s, I could find no reliable reference to it being used in traditional furniture anywhere before then. We know that it isn't traditional, but we don't know why the Halls used it.

One of the obvious features of the drawer joint is that it is made by machine, not by hand. Automatic dovetailing machines were coming into use in the early 20th century, but in a shop the size of the Halls, cutting dovetails by hand would have been the usual method. Although hand-cut dovetails look frightfully complicated and time consuming, an experienced woodworker can make them quickly.

An attempt to make the rabbeted tongue-and-groove joint by hand would probably take longer than dovetailing, even with practice. But with a table saw, this joint is quick to make, and strong enough: the examples from the Hall's shop have held up for nearly 100 years. Was this method used because it was expedient, and is that in character with the other elements of their work?

The volume of work produced in a short period of time suggests a real dedication to efficiency, but the overall quality of that work says that these weren't the kind of craftsmen to cut corners for the sake of speed. Nearly every detail of Greene and Greene furniture is rendered in a way that makes it the best quality possible.

Their methods for making drawers are the only examples in all of their work of them taking the easy way out, but even then, there are details in the drawers that are demanding and time consuming. In some pieces, the top edges of the drawer sides are capped with strips of ebony, attached with what appear to be evenly spaced brass pins. The brass pins, however are actually brass screws, filed down to the point that the slots disappeared after the screws were driven. Men who would carefully file down the heads of dozens of screws to get the look and security of attachment they wanted are not the type of men to choose an unusual joint to save a little time.

The only reason that makes sense to me is that at least one of the four decision-makers involved preferred it, and was able to persuade the others. The Tichenor furniture, made before the Halls, has dovetailed drawers, so we can put the adoption of this method to the time of the Halls. But we don't know if Charles or Henry Greene wanted this detail, or if it originated with Peter or John Hall. The archive drawings don't help to resolve this. In the rare place that drawer details are shown, they are on later drawings, likely prepared so someone other than the Halls could duplicate the original details.

Perhaps the thinking was that furniture was being reinvented. At the time, this furniture was cutting-edge contemporary, and the drawer joint may have been an opportunity to be progressive. The detail may also have come from one of the Halls. Perhaps there was a personal dislike of dovetails, and the chance to do something different was too good to pass up.

This brings us back to the Thorsen house and the question of why not. When I first started considering this, my thinking was that there were two possibilities. The first was that the client insisted on dovetails.

Thorsen was in the lumber business, and was a wealthy and powerful man. He may have held a strong opinion on drawer construction, and as the man paying everyone's salary, he would have had the winning vote.

My other theory is that the cabinetmaker on site made the decision on his own, and that no one realized it until it was too late to scrap the drawers. I like this version, I can picture a stubborn (in my family we call it noble) cabinetmaker who has been making drawers with a joint he doesn't like. Sent north to run the job on his own, he seizes the opportunity to make drawers the "proper" way, willing to gamble that he won't be fired for his independence.

I can't offer any proof of either theory, and the more I considered it, the less likely the rebellious cabinetmaker or the insistent client seemed. I now think the reason is technical, rather than philosophical.

Today when we think of a high-end job site, with skilled craftsmen making furniture in the basement, we assume they would have a table saw. But in 1909, electricity wasn't the given it was today, and in the photos I've seen of the Halls' shop, the table saw is powered by a line shaft, the common method of the day. While they could have shipped the saw to Berkeley, they wouldn't have a way to make it spin when they got there.

My thinking now is that the Thorsen dovetails were made because no one in his right mind would make the rabbeted tongue-and-groove joints by hand. The next logical choice would be the good old dovetail, which any good cabinetmaker of the day would be able to cut in his sleep.

MATERIALS AND FINISHES

Most of the existing Greene and Greene pieces are made of mahogany, with a few notable exceptions. In early pieces for the Tichenor house, ash was used and in the Gamble house, the master and guest bedroom furniture was of walnut and maple. Some pieces like the small stand for the Thorsen house (page 126) were teak. Nearly any quality furniture wood will look good, and contemporary pieces of walnut and cherry are attractive, even if they aren't authentic.

Mahogany was the predominate wood, and for good reason. It has been the premier wood for fine furniture ever since Europeans landed in the new world. It is strong yet easy to work, very stable, displays beautiful figure, and finishes with a wonderful depth and patina. But the mahogany that is available today is not the same material that was available in the early 1900s. At that time, the last remnants of Cuban mahogany were still available, but the supply was beginning to run out.

Cuban mahogany is a close cousin to Honduran and other Central and South American mahoganies and was always considered to be of superior quality. Overcutting is the main reason that it is no longer available. Occasionally some old stock will turn up on the market, but it is priced as a rare commodity and is quite expensive. Both Cuban and Honduran mahogany are today considered commercially extinct.

The availability of the next best thing, big leaf mahogany (*Swietenia macrophylla* which grows throughout Central and South America) varies depending on current political and ecological conditions. There have been moves to place it on endangered species lists, effectively removing it from the marketplace. Like Cuban and Honduran mahogany it has been over-harvested, but the numerous problems of rainforest depletion won't be solved by stopping the trade in one of the most viable, sustainable species.

If you can find big leaf mahogany, which is also sold as genuine mahogany, it will be expensive and of lower quality and smaller sizes than what was available just a few years ago. If you can obtain some, it's probably worthwhile to purchase it as the available substitutes only come close to the appearance and workability. They aren't quite as nice as the real thing, but in a few years there likely won't be any choice in the matter.

African mahogany, *Khaya ivorensis*, is a good choice, having similar appearance, but a coarser and harder structure. The term "mahogany" is applied to a lot of species that look similar to big leaf mahogany but are either not related at all or only distantly related. Philippine mahogany is a good example of this, it has a similar color and some similar properties but it isn't the same material. The world market for hardwoods is constantly in flux and there is little regulation or consistency in what is available. I wouldn't purchase material for furniture construction without seeing it first, and I try to distinguish marketing terms from proper names.

Many exotic woods (a term used to describe non-North American hardwoods) have an attractive figure, but can be very hard on tooling and aren't always stable. Drying practices also vary greatly in different locations so there's a good chance that exotic wood hasn't been dried properly.

Lyptus is a relatively new wood on the scene, developed as a fast growing hybrid. Like many other species it resembles mahogany, but is coarser, harder and only available in smaller sizes. Some users are enthusiastic about it, but I think it's a bit too coarse for fine furniture.

Most of the original Greene and Greene furniture was constructed from solid wood, but there are places where veneered panels were used, and I can't think of any good reasons not to use veneers if that is your preference. If using veneer for a tabletop, a solid wood edge that is thick enough to produce a nicely radiused corner should be applied. If the solid edge is applied to a substrate before the faces are veneered, then the edge can be shaped, and the junction between the solid and the veneer won't be obvious. There is a slight risk, however, that the solid edge will expand in humid conditions, possibly cracking the veneer. Careful selection of seasoned stock will minimize this risk.

So we can't use exactly the same wood that was used in the original furniture, and our ability to use a close substitute is diminishing rapidly. I wish there was an easy answer to this situation, but until the world decides what to do about the tropical rainforests, we are left to do the best that we can with what we have.

If you do manage to find big leaf mahogany, the good news is that it finishes well, and the colors and sheens of original Greene and Greene furniture are not difficult to duplicate. There were three basic tones used, the most familiar and most popular being the rich reddish brown of the Thorsen, Blacker, and Gamble House furniture. Some pieces, like the Freeman Ford furniture and the Charles Greene sideboard, are a dark brown, and the Bolton/Bush and Culbertson pieces are nearly black.

One of the interesting finds within the Virtual Archives is a recipe for the color from the Thorsen house. This was written by Charles Greene in the 1920s so that some newer work could match the original. There is also a handwritten note from Greene to Thorsen that explains how he obtained the color, and advising Thorsen that any decent painter should be able to understand and use it.

I have used this method and it works very well, producing a wonderful color and luminescence. The first step is to treat the wood with a solution of potassium dichromate. This chemical should be used cautiously; it has the distinction of being both a carcinogen and a toxin. It comes in powdered form, about half an ounce dissolved in a quart of distilled water will produce good results. Wear a respirator (not a dust mask) while handling the powder, and wear rubber gloves and goggles while working with the liquid solution. Be sure to get, read and follow the information contained in the Material Safety Data Sheet for this material.

It is a strong oxidizer, and brushing it on the wood will turn the wood a rusty orange-red color. The best technique is to apply it to the wood with a brush and then wipe the surface dry within a few minutes. Puddles left on a surface, or excess liquid collecting in corners will darken those areas excessively.

After the potassium dichromate solution has been left to dry for a day or two, the wood can be stained with artist's oil colors dissolved in Danish oil or boiled linseed oil. The Charles Greene recipe for the Thorsen house called for:

$3\frac{1}{2}$ parts chrome yellow
3 parts raw umber
$2\frac{5}{8}$ parts white lead and
$\frac{1}{8}$ part sylvan green

At an artist's supply store you can find tubes of oil colors in different sizes. The smallest ones should provide enough color to make a batch of stain for one or two pieces of furniture. Chrome yellow and raw umber are still available, but white lead has been replaced by titanium white. I haven't been able to find sylvan green, but since it is such a small part of the mixture, I substituted hooker's green.

To mix the colors, I squeezed a line from each tube on to a piece of scrap plywood, taking one "part" as a line 2 inches long. Thus the chrome yellow was a line 7 inches long, the raw umber a line 6 inches long, etc. Mix the colors together to blend them, and then put that mixture into a pint of Danish oil. It takes a good deal of stirring to get the colors completely dissolved, but this makes an effective and simple-to-use stain.

It is a bilious green color, but this counteracts the burnt orange from the chemical treatment and the end result is beautiful. I wipe the stain on liberally, let it sit for ten or fifteen minutes, then wipe the excess off the surface. Other colors can be achieved by mixing different combinations of artist's oils. I use Danish oil as a topcoat, which is similar in effect to the original finishes. Satin finish lacquer will give a similar finished appearance.

The darker brown colors are very similar to many commercially available stains, generally, those described as walnut. Test colors on scraps from the project before committing to any stain color or application method.

References I have found to the original finishes always refer to "oil" which I assume is boiled linseed oil. Original finishes are not filled, the grain and pores of the wood are apparent, and the sheen is satin. Although only a few coats of oil were likely applied when the furniture was new, it was well cared for and likely waxed or re-oiled on a regular basis. Henry Greene took responsibility for maintaining the interiors of some of the houses around Pasadena in his later years. There is a letter from him to Charles written in the late 1930s that comments on how well the Blacker house looks after receiving a thorough "going over."

After treating the wood with a potassium dichromate solution, a green stain is applied. The stain is mixed by adding artist's oil colors to a base of Danish oil.

After leaving the stain for 10-15 minutes, the excess is wiped from the surface. Green and red are opposites on a color wheel and the stain mellows the reddish-orange tendencies of the chemical treatment, leaving a beautiful, luminescent color.

THE DRAWINGS

The drawings in this book are the first published detail drawings of the furniture designed by Charles and Henry Greene and built by Peter and John Hall. There is a tradition of books like this, going back to the work of Wallace Nutting in America in the 1920s, and even further back to books like Thomas Chippendale's "The Gentleman and Cabinetmakers Director" originally published in 1762. For anyone interested in the design and construction of furniture this is an invaluable resource, but for those unfamiliar with reading construction drawings, some explanation is in order.

These drawings are as close as I can come to the actual pieces, but there were some serious constraints on my research that prevent them from being perfect. Access to original pieces was very limited. I was only given brief amounts of time, and wasn't allowed to measure or take photographs. The Huntington Museum allows photography but the lights are dim, and they don't allow the use of tripods or supplemental lighting. I studied the archived drawings, but these don't really show construction details and in almost every piece, there are significant deviations between the drawing and the finished furniture.

I did a lot of research, spent a lot of time sketching original pieces, spent countless hours staring at photographs, worrying over details and talking about them with other woodworkers. This was an exercise in problem solving, working from known information to derive the unknown. There are places where I had to make a good guess, and I'm sure there are details I have missed. I hope this work will be judged for its usefulness, not its lack of perfection.

Mechanical drawing is the language of construction: the way of communicating the designer's intent to the person actually doing the work. Like any language, there are some quirks and idiosyncrasies that aren't ready apparent to the uninitiated. In the 1960's when I was in high school, it was still common for everyone, at least the males, to take at least one class in mechanical drawing as well as one class in wood and metal shop. This has changed over the last 40 years, and as a consequence the connection has been broken between the common man and the way the world is built.

The views in these drawings are mechanical, that is, they are made from a point of view that is at a perfect right angle to the top, side, or front of the object. The beauty of this is that the relationship between the parts can be observed and measured, distances can be accurately calculated, and the sequence of work can be planned. The hurdle most people struggle to get over is that not all of the information about an object can be shown in any one view. Because it is a two-dimensional pattern rather than a three-dimensional rendering, the best you can do is show two thirds of the information in any one view.

In real life, and in illustrative drawing, perspective comes into play. The point of view and angle of view let you see all of the front and parts of the top and side. The proportions and sizes of parts of the object will seem to vary as the point of view shifts. This gives you a good idea of the overall appearance of something, but measuring and determining the relationships between parts is quite difficult.

To know all you need to know to build

something from a mechanical drawing, you need to develop the ability to locate pieces in two or more views and correlate the information. A quick glance isn't enough, you need to look, question, seek and find elements of the piece, to be able to build it. Studying a drawing leads you to the exercise of mentally building before physically building. Other forms of drawing may look prettier on the page, but they make precise work more difficult.

I feel fortunate that I was taught to draw with a pencil, T-square and triangles before learning how to draw in AutoCAD. It is very much a process of problem solving, and there are specific ways that drawings are prepared that lead the builder to solve the problems before the building begins. As a cabinetmaker, I know that going directly from a drawing to cutting wood is an invitation to disaster. There needs to be some time in between, a time of planning, determining the sizes of parts, making decisions about joining techniques and the sequence of work. These are vital skills for an accomplished cabinetmaker to possess, and I'm from the school of thought that it's better to teach someone how to fish and feed him for a lifetime rather than to give him a fish and only feed him for today.

Some of the comments on my earlier books were that there were no step-by-step instructions and that you really needed to study the drawings before you could build from them. You had to hunt to find all the dimensions you needed, and sometimes you actually had to add or subtract. I think these were intended as criticism, but I took them as compliments. I was taught to prepare a drawing so that the person reading it needed to look at every view. If it seems that some information is missing, go back and look at the other views or detail drawings. There are good reasons for showing different views and details.

One of the other things I was taught is that it is important to make the builder calculate and double-check the dimensions. This is from the days when dimensions were calculated with pencil and paper, before computer software could automatically generate accurate dimensions. People aren't perfect, and while I have done the best that I can to generate accurate drawings, I am perfectly capable of making mistakes. There are also points in the production of a book like this where dimensions generated by AutoCAD need to be converted by another program, and this is another place where errors can creep in. A good builder will catch an error in a drawing and correct for it before beginning to build.

This is why there are no parts lists or cutting diagrams in this book. The furniture presented here is complex, and it deserves the careful attention of anyone attempting to reproduce it. It's not the kind of stuff that you can assemble from a stack of pre-cut parts. There will be many decisions along the way that only the builder can make, and these decisions will affect the overall sizes of parts, and the sizes of adjacent parts. After a closer look at the elements of the drawings, I will present the procedure I follow and recommend for you to build from them.

The drawings that look directly at the front and side of a piece are called elevations. These represent the outside of the finished piece, but they can't tell the story of what is going on inside. Where dashed lines appear in an elevation, they represent something important that is hidden from view. In most of the drawings in this book, dashed lines in elevations show the extent of the joints that connect the parts seen in the elevations.

To show what is going on inside the piece, a different kind of drawing, called a section, is presented. A section shows

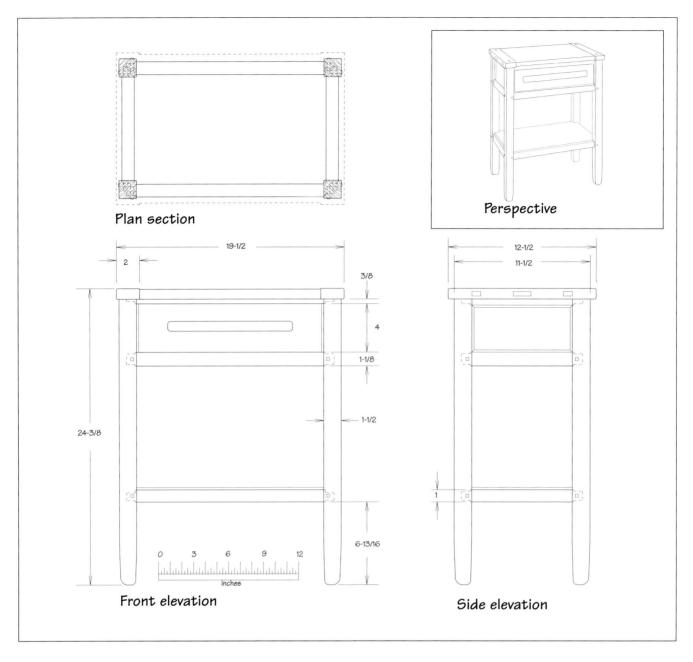

Plan section

Perspective

19-1/2

2

3/8

4

1-1/8

1-1/2

24-3/8

6-13/16

0   3   6   9   12

inches

Front elevation

12-1/2

11-1/2

1

Side elevation

what it would look like if you made a perfect vertical or horizontal cut through the piece of furniture, and discarded everything on the viewer's side of that cut. This imaginary cut is called a cutting line or cutting plane. If you cut a sandwich in half, throw away one half and look at where the cut was made, you have a real life example of the imaginary cut made to produce a section drawing.

In a section drawing, the parts that are on the cutting plane are filled in with a pattern that represents the material it is made

of, in most cases in these drawings, solid wood. Different patterns will show plywood, glass, or other material. Parts that are beyond the cutting plane are shown by thinner lines than those of the parts that are cut. Parts that are on the viewer's side of the cutting plane are shown as dashed lines. If there isn't an indication on the elevation drawings of the location of the cutting plane, it can be assumed that it is in the center of the elevation.

Plan views look straight down on the object, and the majority of plan views in this book are actually plan sections. The main portion of the drawing will show the location and relationship of legs and rails, and the dashed lines will indicate the location of the top of the piece.

One of the disadvantages of drawings reproduced in a book is that they must be scaled down to fit on the page. In a cabinet shop or furniture factory, drawings are printed on larger format paper, usually 18" x 24" or 24" x 36". It's easier to organize the drawing in a larger format, and details can be shown in a larger scale. There is also a lot more space to put dimensions in a large format drawing.

One of the rules of drafting that I was taught is that the dimension of any given part should appear only once in the drawing, and in the location where it makes the most sense to appear. The length of a horizontal rail will be found as a horizontal dimension in an elevation, and the width and thickness will appear in a section view. If a dimension seems to be missing, look for it in a different view, or it may need to be calculated from the dimension of other parts.

For many of the close details in this book, separate detail drawings have been included. Due to the limits of space, however, there isn't always room to dimension every part and its' location. In these instances, a scale has been included with the detail drawing. You can make marks on a piece of scrap paper or index card held against the drawing, or use a pair of dividers, to pick the size of a part from the detail drawing and compare that to the scale to determine its' actual size.

In real life shop drawings, the drawings are all at a standard scale where $1/2$ inch, 1 inch, $1^1/2$ inch, or 3 inch equals one foot. Triangular shaped architect's and engineer's rules are made with these different

scales on different edges, and sizes can be determined by measuring the drawing with these scales. For the shapes of curved parts, there are detail drawings on a grid of squares. Where this appears, there will be a note giving the actual size of the squares.

Before computers and photocopiers, the way to generate these curves was to draw the grid at full-size on paper or thin plywood, note the locations where the curved lines crossed the grid on the drawing, and transfer those point locations to the full-size grid. When the points have been located on the full size grid, they can be connected by sketching in curves that contain them. This still works, but many copy centers will have a machine capable of scaling a small drawing up in size. Make a copy larger than the page in the book, measure the space between the lines on the grid, and calculate how much larger or smaller the next copy must be scaled to reach the stated dimension. When you get the scaling right, make a spare copy or two. You can stick these onto template material, cut to the lines on the copied drawing, and save yourself a great deal of time.

A vigilant employee at the copy shop will likely tell you that this book is copyrighted material and that you can't make copies without the permission of the copyright holder. You can show them this paragraph. As the author and copyright holder, I greatly appreciate your watching out for my rights. It's OK with me if you copy and blow up a few pages to generate full size patterns. It's not OK to copy the whole book and sell it on eBay.

So how does one get from the drawing to the pile of parts that will make a finished piece of furniture? If the drawing is accurate, why wouldn't it be a good idea to make a list, cut all the parts to finished size, make all the joints and put the thing together? That sounds like the easy way, and it sure would save a lot of time.

I have been building furniture and cabinets and preparing drawings for a long time. I believe, and have been told by people whose opinions I respect, that my drawings are very good. I have prepared drawings for architectural projects that represent hundreds of thousands of dollars worth of work. I'm pretty confident in my ability to generate an accurate, buildable drawing. But when I walk out into the shop to build something from one of my own drawings I prove every line and every dimension before I start, and I don't cut pieces to their final size or make any joints until I am absolutely certain that it will be right.

I'll make a full size layout of the major components on a scrap piece of wood, and if I'm not sure how a joint will go together, I will make one or two for practice. If I was so confident just a paragraph ago, why do I do all this extra work? The reason is: this isn't extra work. It's a common-sense method of building that has been used for centuries, it is more efficient, and it produces better quality work.

Working from the drawing, I make a cutting list and double check all the numbers. I start with the biggest pieces, work to the smallest, and list the finished sizes on a piece of paper. When I select the lumber and start cutting parts my list is organized so that I have the most wood to choose from for the largest, most visible parts. I cut everything larger than I need for two reasons.

The first is that solid wood often moves or distorts in the first day or two after being cut. Leaving it big to begin with lets me make better parts if this happens, and better parts make better furniture. The second reason is that every part of a piece of furniture is related to every other part. If for some reason a piece changes slightly in size early on, it can change the spacing or the size of every other piece. If I leave the pieces over sized as long as I can, it's insurance against small errors accumulating and creating a nightmare at the end.

I like to make story poles, life size section drawings of how the parts fit and relate to each other. This is like a practice run, making sure I'm happy with the sequence of work I've planned, and the way I plan on doing things. It also saves a lot of time measuring, marking, and calculating. I can compare my parts to the story pole, double-check my work, and mark joint layouts from the pole instead of measuring each and every piece.

I also like to plan subassemblies. I've yet to see a piece of furniture that was completely assembled in one step. A minor deviation in one of the subassemblies or one of its components can be compensated for if the remaining parts for the next step are still oversized. Making furniture one piece at a time isn't the same process as making furniture in a factory, so I try to avoid thinking like a factory manager. I still strive to work efficiently, but making one piece at a time also demands some flexibility. The most inefficient thing is to make something twice because I rushed ahead without thinking it through.

RESOURCES

Fortunately for us, the Greene brothers were packrats and many of their original drawings, correspondence, photographs and other material has been preserved. Much of this material is available online at the Greene and Greene Virtual Archives, http://www.usc.edu/dept/architecture/greeneandgreene/index.html. The archive features thousands of documents.

The existing homes and furniture pieces that are available for public viewing are concentrated in the Los Angeles area. The Los Angeles County Museum of Art has several pieces, but the best destinations are the Gamble House in Pasadena, and the Scott Gallery at the Huntington Museum in San Marino.

The Gamble House is in near original condition, and most of the furniture can be seen where it was originally placed. The general tour is a little hurried, so if you're really interested in the furniture try to join a slower "behind the velvet ropes" tour.

The Huntington Collection contains a re-creation of the Robinson House dining room with the original furniture, several pieces from the Thorsen, Freeman Ford, Blacker, and Culbertson houses, and the massive sideboard that was made for Charles Greene in 1913.

There are a number of books on the work of the brothers, but other than this one, only two specifically deal with the furniture. Randall Makinson's *Furniture and Related Designs* contains a great deal of information, although his point of view is that of an architect and collector, rather than a cabinetmaker. Darrell Peart's *Greene and Greene: Design Details for the Workshop* is a welcome addition, written from the enthusiastic point of view of a good maker.

The most reliable and informative book that takes a broad look at the entire career of Charles and Henry Greene is Edward R. Bosley's *Greene and Greene*. Bosley is the director of the Gamble House, a thorough researcher, and an excellent writer.

A good overview of the furniture of the Arts & Crafts period is *Arts & Crafts Furniture, from Classic to Contemporary* by Kevin Rodel and Jon Binzen, written by furniture makers, and so more furniture-friendly than most works on the period.

There are a lot of other books on the Greenes that are useful as visual resources, but short on scholarship and practical information. I'm not generally a fan of coffee table books but seeing complete interiors and the furniture in context makes most of these worthwhile. One of the best of the bunch is *Images of the Gamble House Masterwork of Greene and Greene by* Jeanette A. Thomas.

Further reading

Randell L. Makinson:

Greene & Greene: Architecture as Fine Art, Gibbs Smith publishers, ISBN 0879051264.

Greene & Greene: Creating a Style, Gibbs Smith, ISBN 1586851160.

The Blacker House, Gibbs Smith publishers, ISBN 0879059494.

Marvin Rand: *Greene and Greene*, Gibbs Smith publishers, ISBN 1586854453.

Bruce Smith and Alexander Vertikoff: *Greene and Greene: Masterworks*, Chronicle Books, ISBN: 0811818780.

George Ellis: *Modern Practical Joinery*, Linden Publishing, ISBN 0941936082.

Bernard Jones, Ed.: *The Complete Woodworker*, Ten Speed Press, ISBN 0898150221.

Gamble House chiffonier.

Photo: Ognan Borissov, Interfoto

GAMBLE CHIFFONIER

This inlaid walnut bedroom case is one of the most detailed pieces in the house, and part of the master bedroom suite that included two beds, a bureau, a desk, a taborette and several chairs. This was the most expensive piece of furniture in the house, costing $680.38. That sounds like a bargain, but at the time the Halls were billing their labor at fifty cents per hour. The $578.20 for labor in this piece represents over 1,150 hours. In today's market for custom furniture the price to make this piece would likely be close to $70,000.

The carved inlay on the doors and mirror rail would take a significant amount of those hours, but the box-jointed drawers, carved pulls and other details are also time consuming. The box joints increase in size from the top of the case to the bottom, making the joinery even more time consuming. The entire bedroom suite was billed at $2743.36 , almost 5,500 man hours of shop time. The statement in the archive indicates that the first bill for the furniture was "put to Mr. Gamble" in November 1908, and that most of the furniture was complete by the end of August 1909.

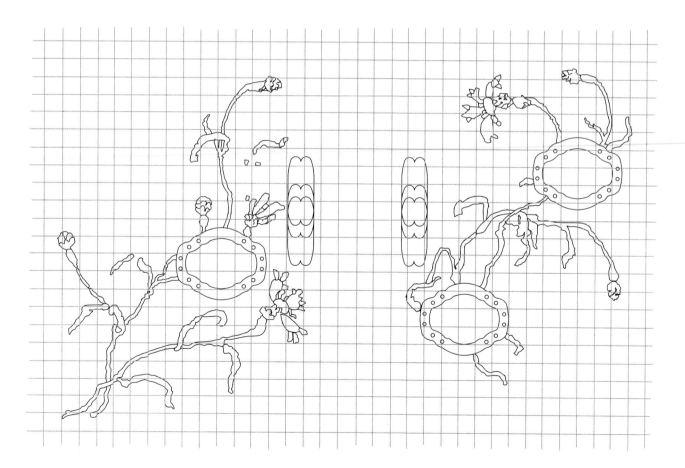

Inlay detail, Gamble House chiffonier

grid = ½" squares

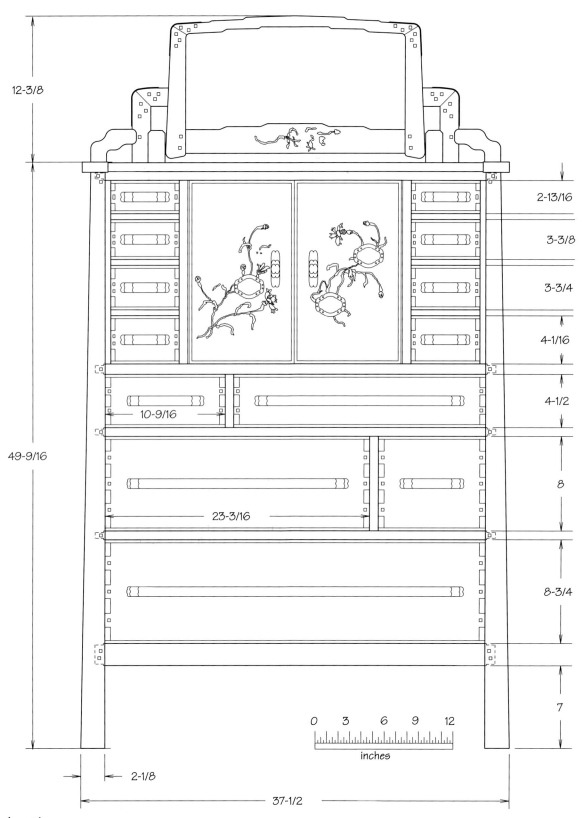

12-3/8

2-13/16

3-3/8

3-3/4

4-1/16

4-1/2

49-9/16

10-9/16

8

23-3/16

8-3/4

0   3   6   9   12

inches

7

2-1/8

37-1/2

Front elevation

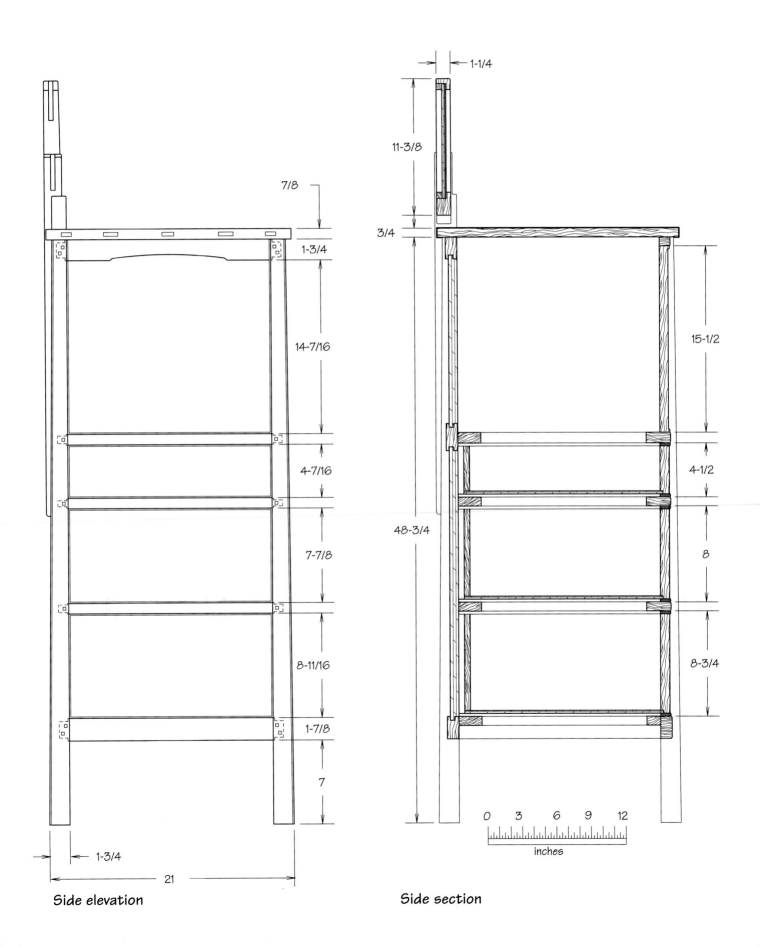

Side elevation

Side section

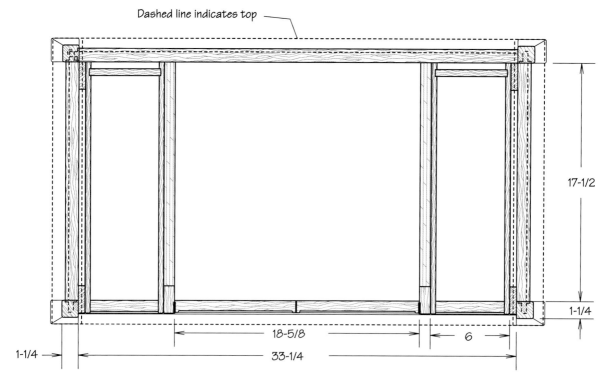

Dashed line indicates top

17-1/2

1-1/4

18-5/8

33-1/4

6

1-1/4

Plan section through cupboard

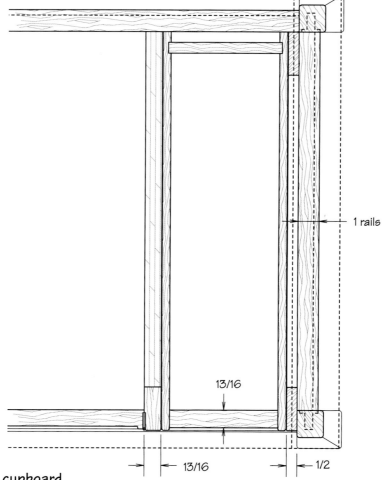

1 rails

13/16

13/16

1/2

Plan section through cupboard

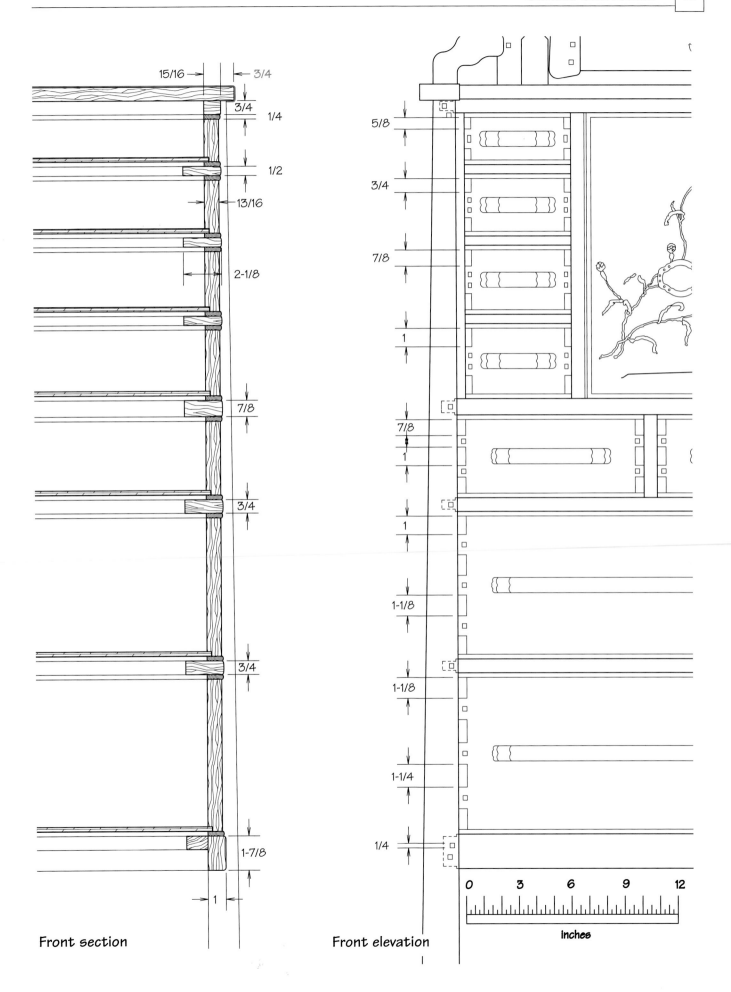

Front section

Front elevation

Inches

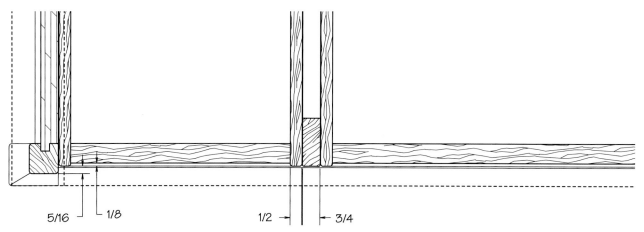

Plan section through drawer

5/16   1/8   1/2   3/4

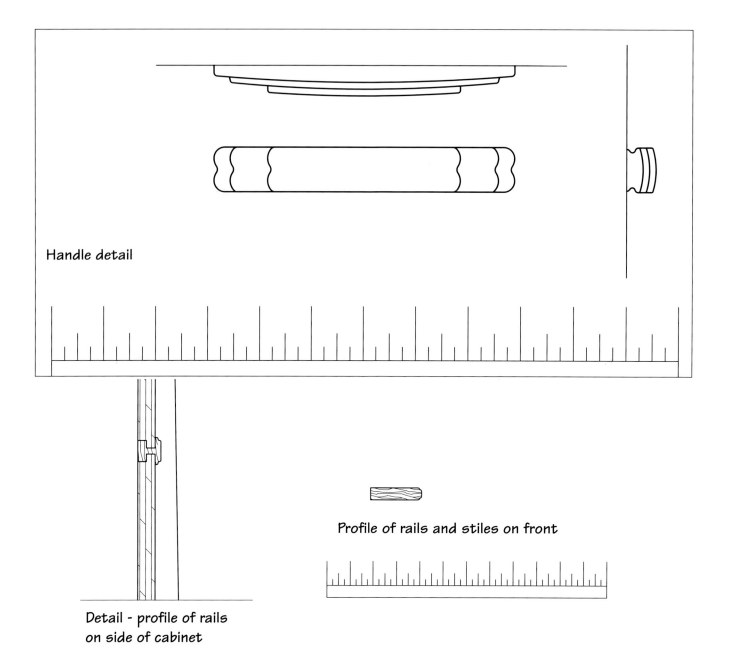

Handle detail

Detail - profile of rails
on side of cabinet

Profile of rails and stiles on front

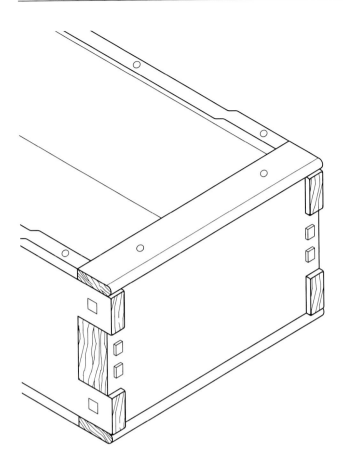

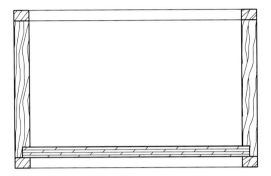

Front section through drawer

Drawer details

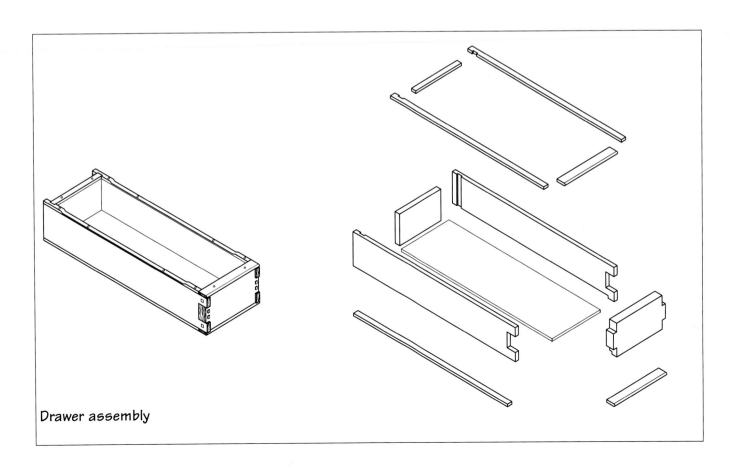

Drawer assembly

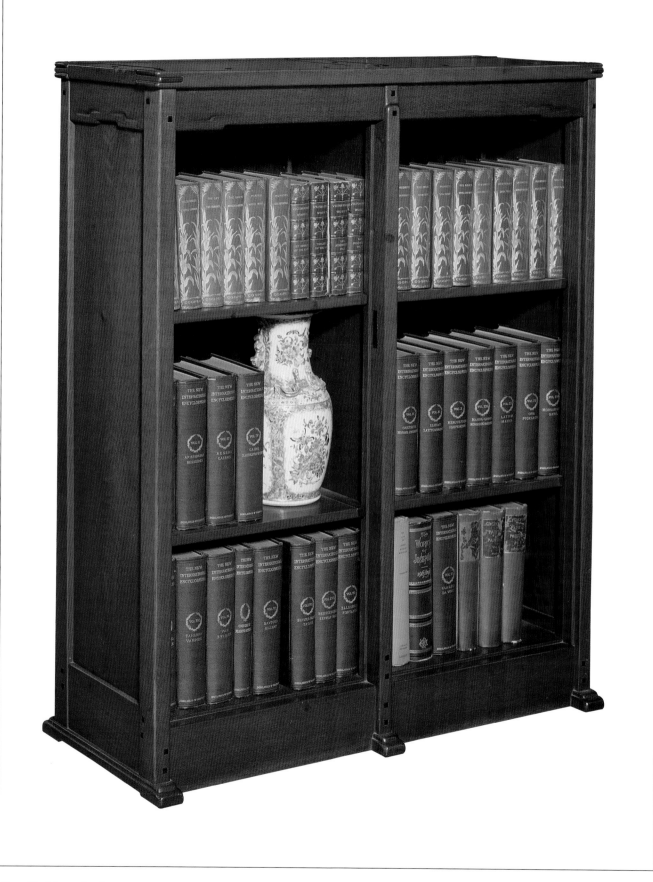

Gamble House bookcase.

Photo: Ognan Borissov, Interfoto

GAMBLE BOOKCASE

There are two of these bookcases in the Gamble house living room, this is the smaller of the two and is just off the main entry hall. The larger version has three vertical sections and sits diagonally opposite in the room. Like all of the Gamble furniture, there are some intricate and unusual details.

The panels in the top of the case are raised, The reversing curved profile of these panels is unusual, and was likely produced with a custom ground shaper cutter. Raised panels don't occur often in Greene and Greene furniture, and the profile is

actually close to one commonly used in solid wood drawer bottoms. The stiles and rails surrounding these panels are joined with a bridle joint, the center of the joint aligning with the groove for the panels. The plug pattern on top suggests that the top is held to the case with screws hidden by the ebony plugs.

The lightning bolt shapes on the top rails are carved, approximately $1/8$ inch deep. The pins that hold the shelves in place are small cubes of ebony, and the shelves are fitted with breadboard end.

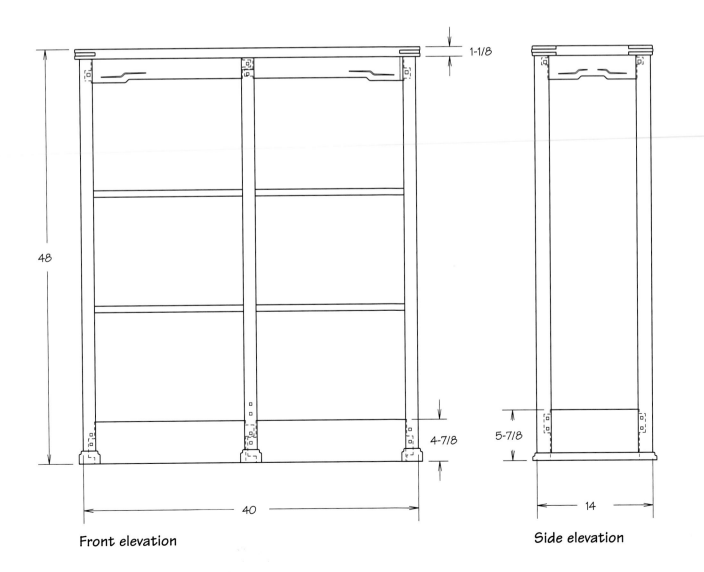

Front elevation

Side elevation

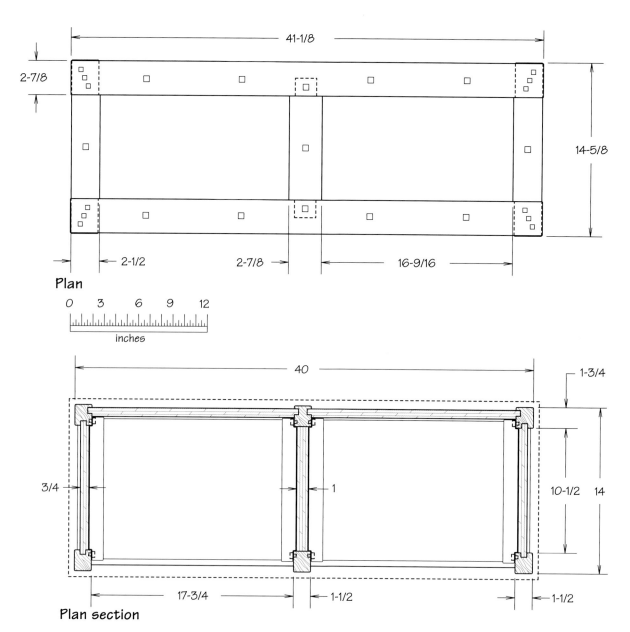

Plan

0   3   6   9   12
inches

Plan section

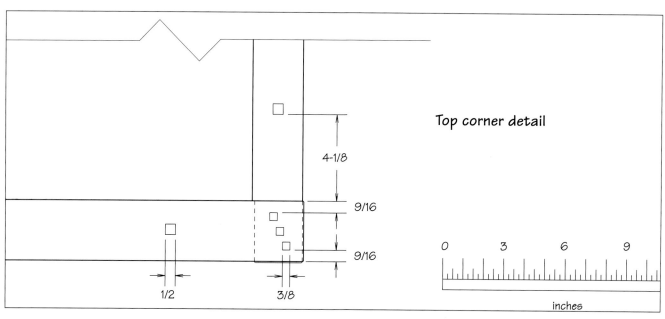

Top corner detail

0   3   6   9
inches

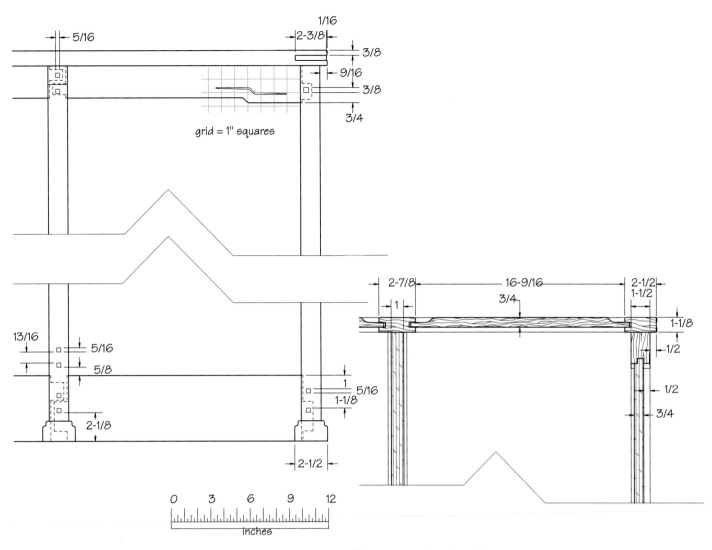

grid = 1" squares

0   3   6   9   12
inches

Front elevation details

Front section details

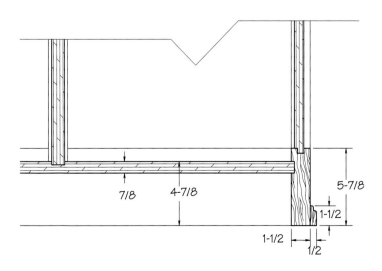

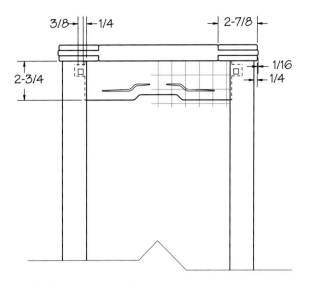

Side elevation details

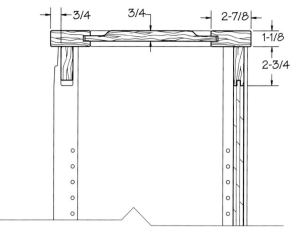

Side section details

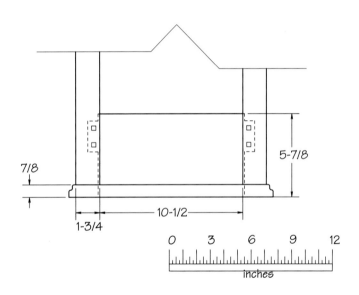

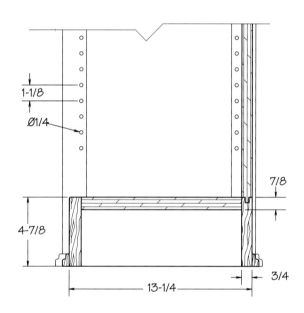

inches

FREEMAN FORD SERVING TABLE

When I first made a reproduction of this piece for *Popular Woodworking* magazine, I hadn't seen the original, but worked from an archive photograph. This drawing is a more accurate depiction of this unusual table. The legs are subtly sculpted, hollow between the edges and gently rounded on the edges.

The top is offset from the base, and features delicate inlays at either end. The inlays are realistically carved, and sit slightly proud of the top's surface. The Ford furniture has a slightly darker finish than is usually seen, more brown than red.

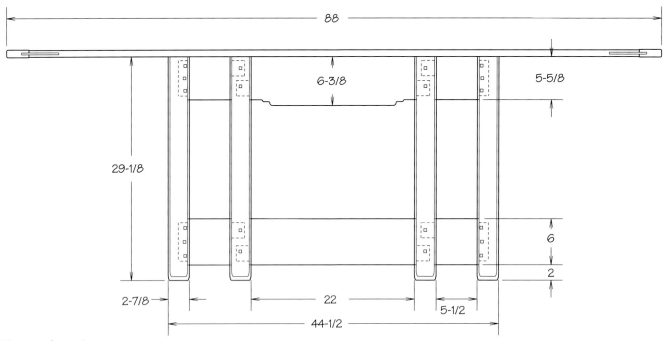

Front elevation

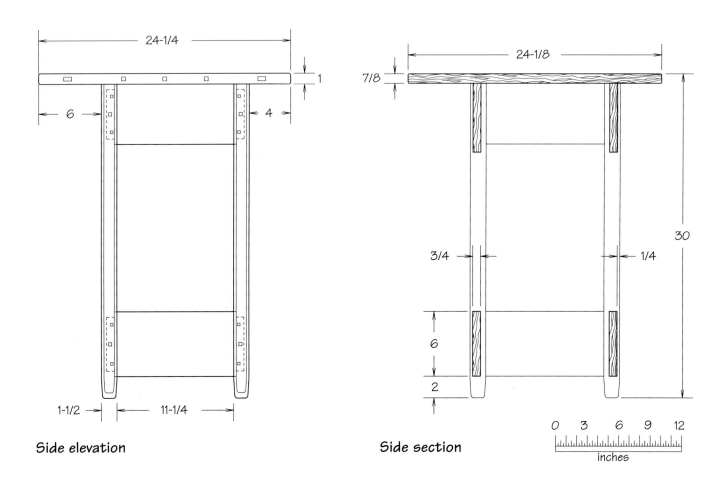

Side elevation

Side section

inches

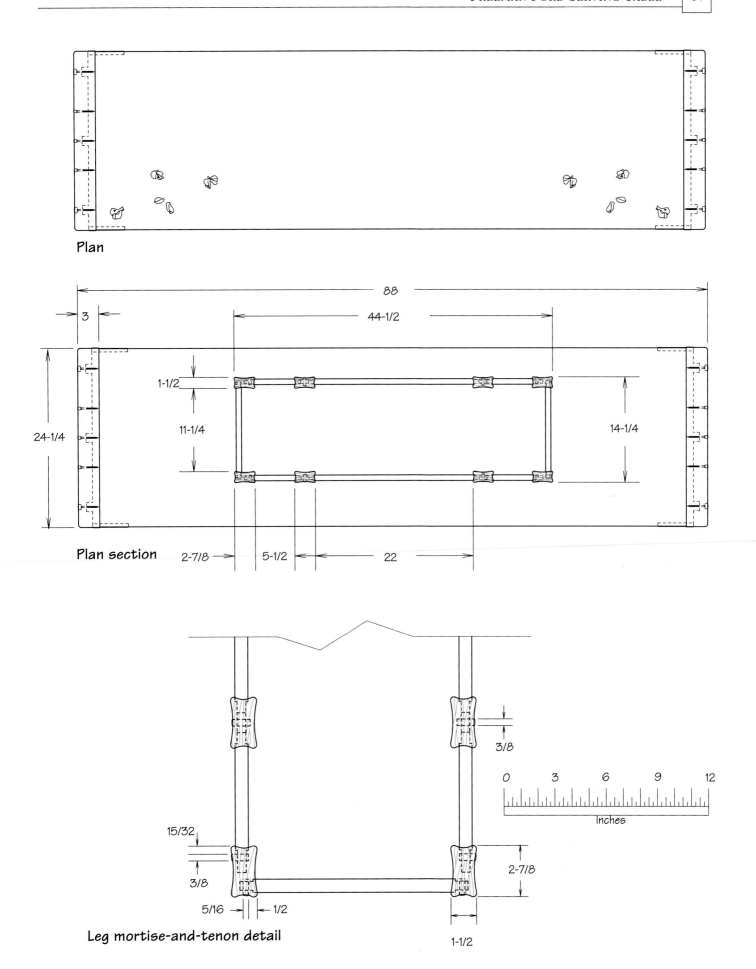

Plan

Plan section

Leg mortise-and-tenon detail

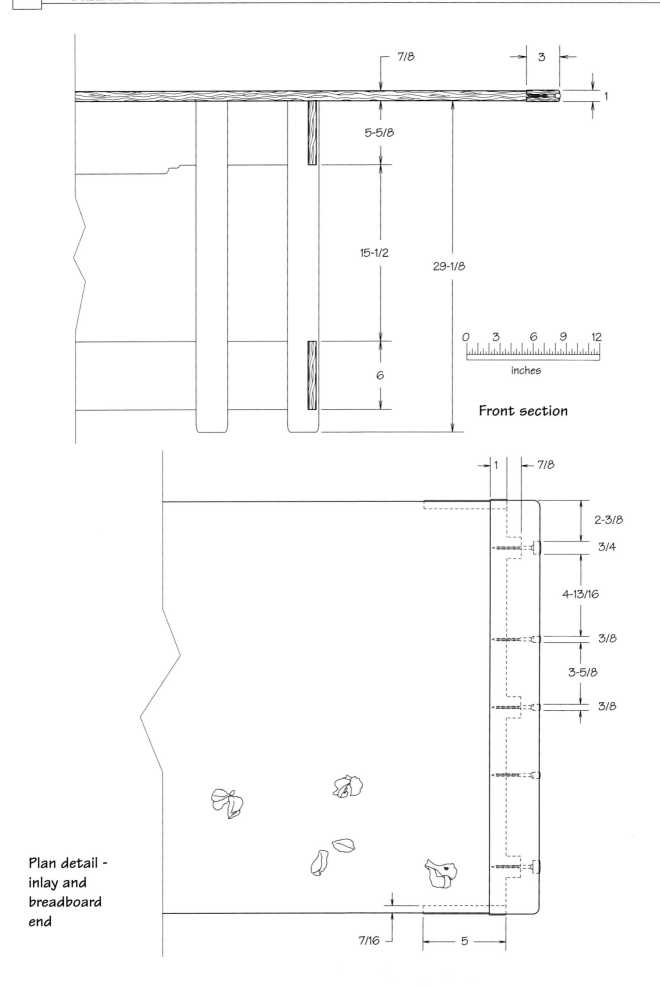

7/8

3

1

5-5/8

15-1/2

29-1/8

6

0   3   6   9   12

inches

Front section

1

7/8

2-3/8

3/4

4-13/16

3/8

3-5/8

3/8

**Plan detail -
inlay and
breadboard
end**

7/16

5

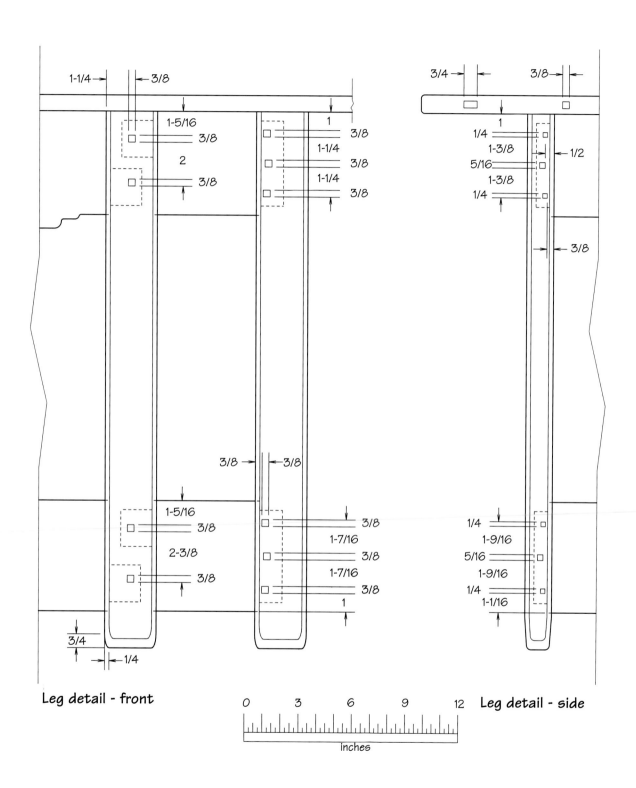

Leg detail - front

Leg detail - side

0   3   6   9   12
inches

Thorsen House serving table, now at the Huntington Museum, Los Angeles   *Photo: Ognan Borissov, Interfoto*

THORSEN SERVING TABLE

The Thorsen House is in Berkeley, several hundred miles away from the Pasadena home of the Hall brothers shop. Only the dining room furniture was part of the original commission, and workers were sent to the job site to assemble the furniture in the basement of the house. There were also several wonderful built-ins in the Thorsen House, so it made sense to do all of this work on site. Whether the men on site built the furniture from scratch, or only assembled parts prepared in the mill in Pasadena, isn't known.

In addition to the inlays and horizontal cuts in the rails, one of the interesting features of the Thorsen work is the construction of the drawers. It is the only known example of work for the Greenes by the Halls that contained dovetailed drawer construction.

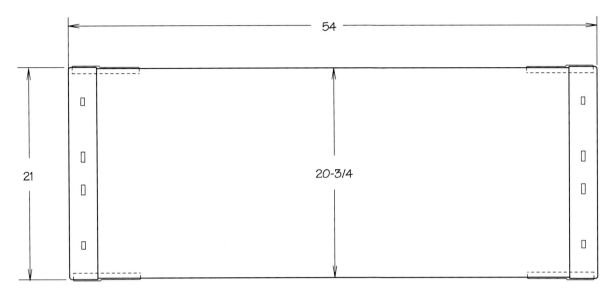

Plan

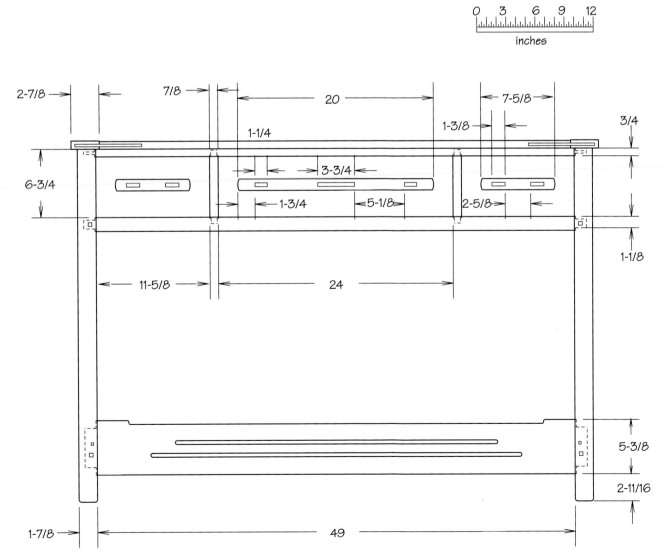

Front elevation

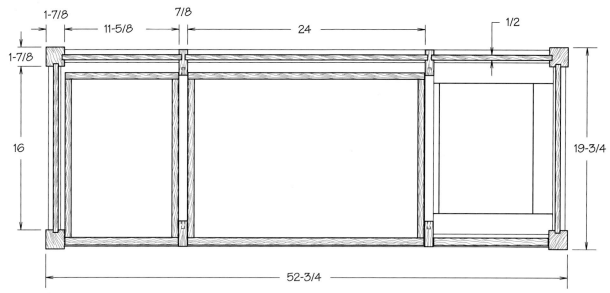

Plan section

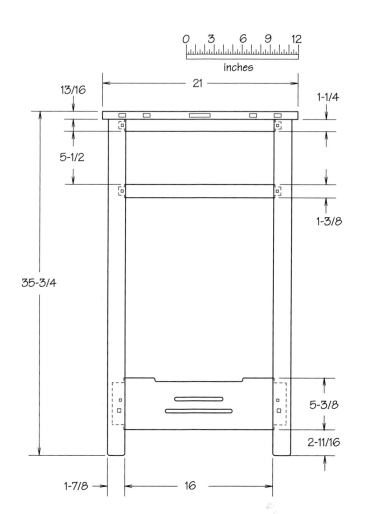

Side elevation

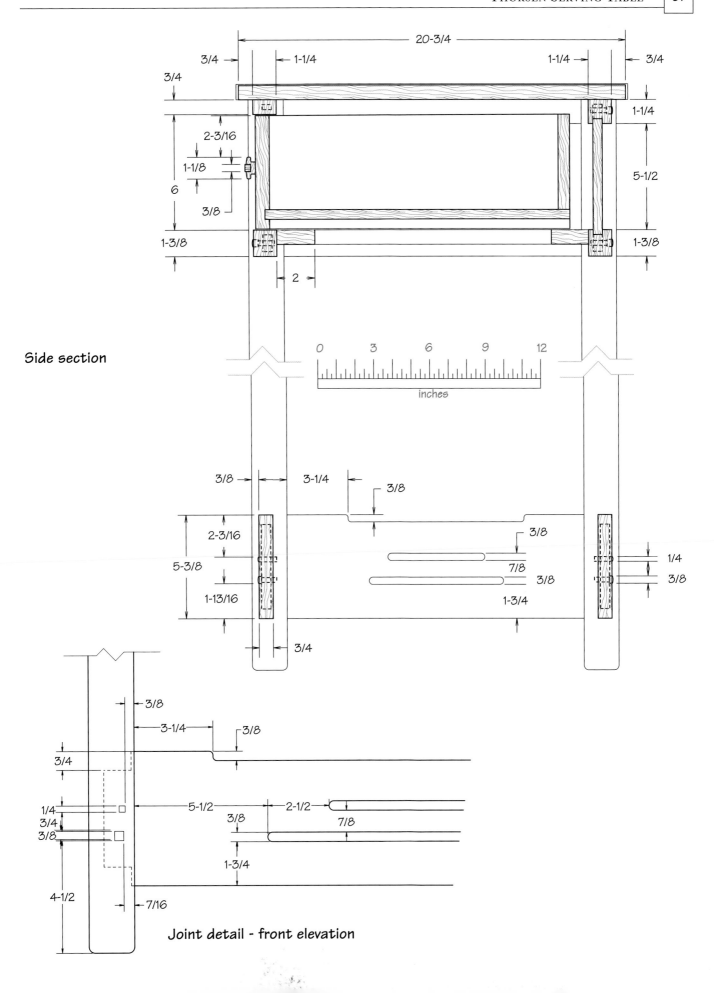

Side section

inches

Joint detail - front elevation

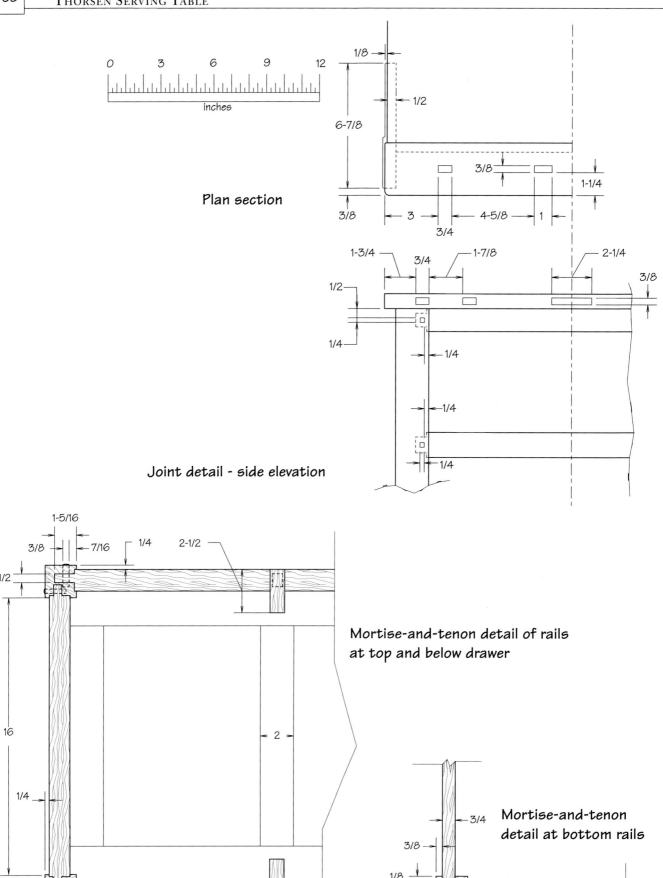

Plan section

Joint detail - side elevation

Mortise-and-tenon detail of rails
at top and below drawer

Mortise-and-tenon
detail at bottom rails

Gamble House entry table

Photo: Ognan Borissov, Interfoto

GAMBLE ENTRY TABLE

The front entry hall to the Gamble House is an enchanted place, especially in the morning when the sun hits the art glass on the front doors, and the space is bathed is a glowing yellow light. To the right of the front door is the stairway, and to the left is a long wall with this table, flanked by two large armchairs as its centerpiece. One of the most notable features of this piece is the drawer.

Held together at the corners with a proud, sculpted box joint, the drawer slides in and out on ebony slides that are attached to the top of the drawer sides, and fit in with a narrow ebony strip that runs across the front of the table. These slides appear to be held to the drawer with small brass pins. The brass pins are actually screws that have had their heads filed off below the level of the slots. The small ebony knob on the back of the drawer has an inlaid mother of pearl dot at the center. It hits the wall as the drawer is closed, keeping the drawer centered front to back.

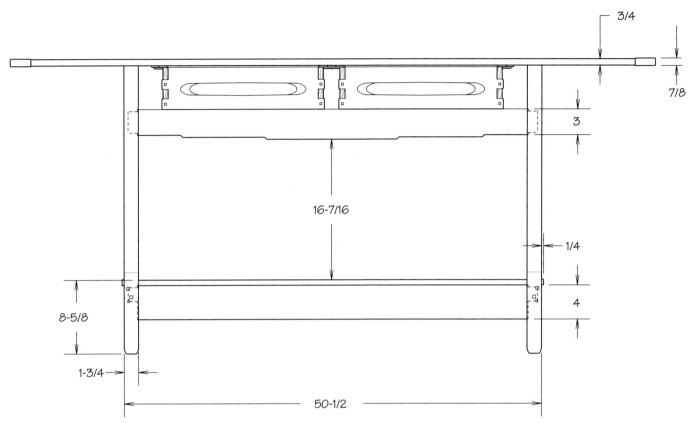

Front elevation

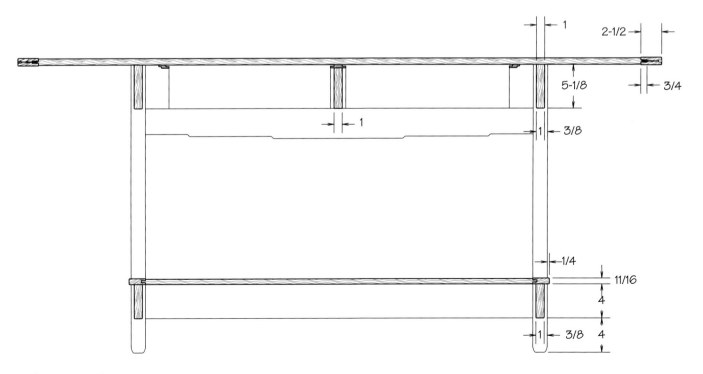

Front section

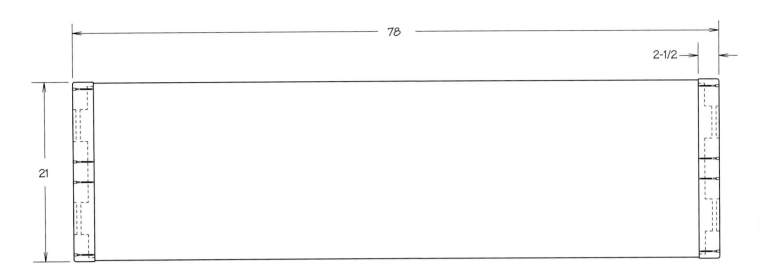

Plan

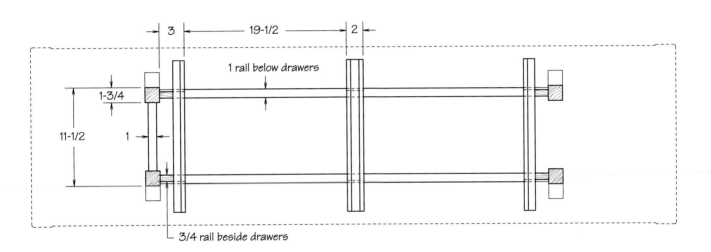

Plan section

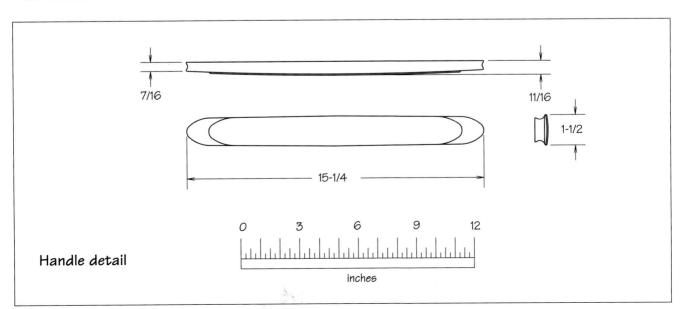

Handle detail

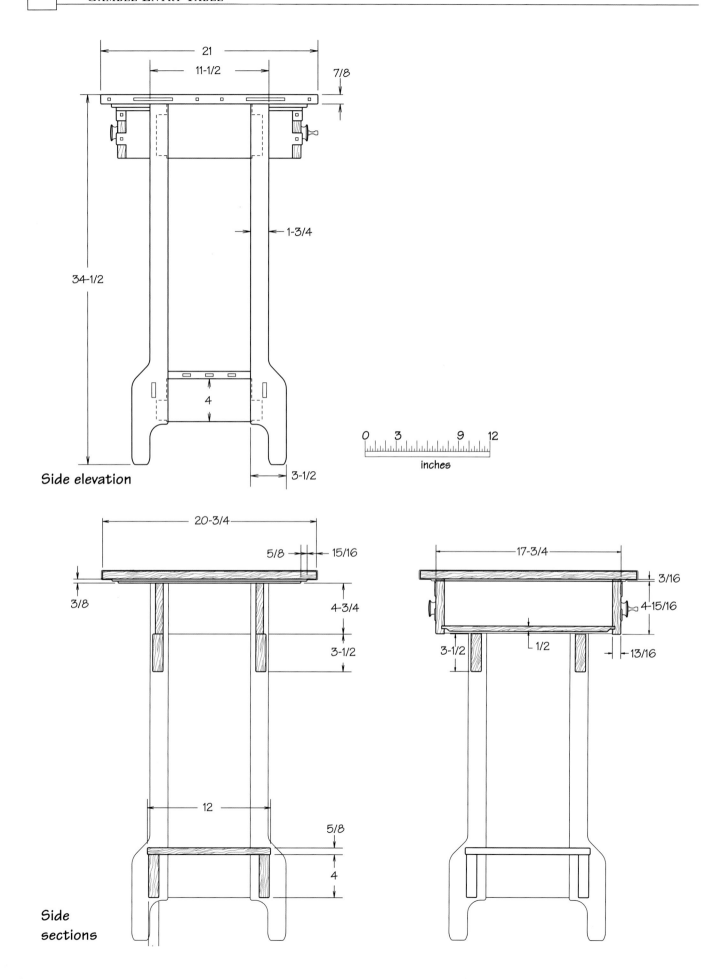

Side elevation

Side
sections

inches

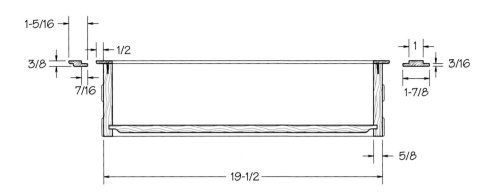

Drawer and slide detail

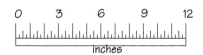

inches

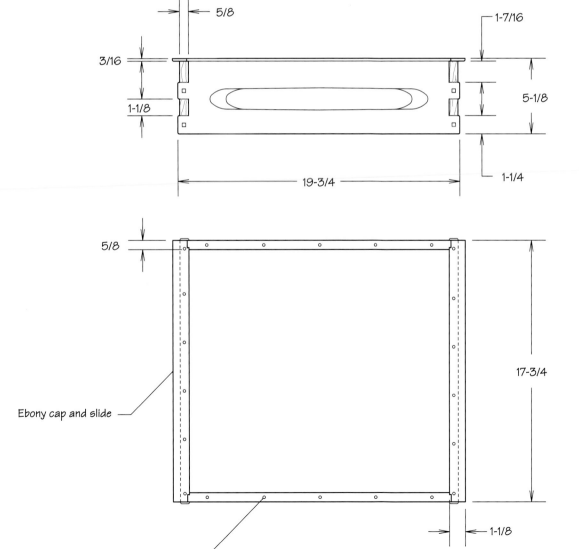

Ebony cap and slide

Brass pins

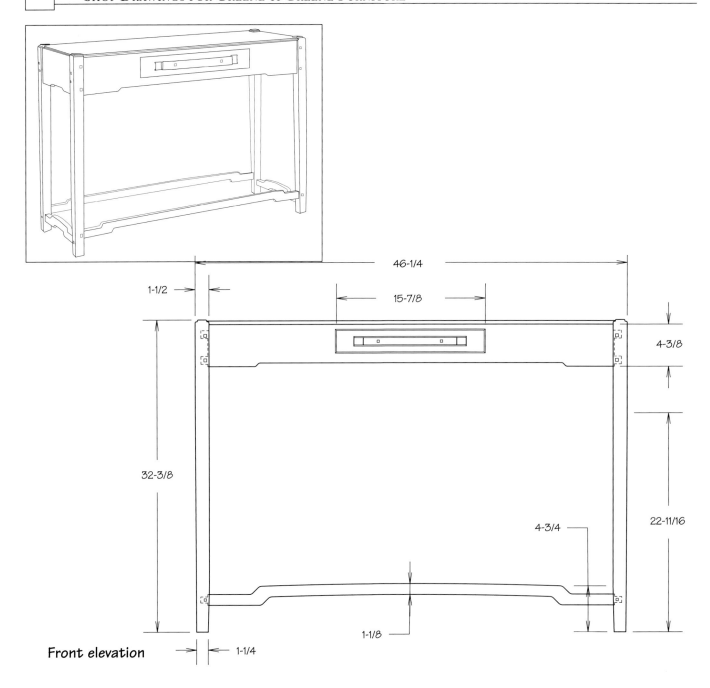

Front elevation

BOLTON HALL TABLE

This table sat between two high-backed chairs in the Bolton entry, and shares some of the chair details, notably the shaping of the top of the legs, and the cloud-lift rails. The shaping of the legs and the carving on the drawer pull make this a delicate and refined piece. The finish color on these pieces was among the darkest used, and after nearly a century is today almost black.

Dr. William Bolton was a long-term client of the Greenes; this furniture is from the third house he commissioned in less than 10 years. Dr. Bolton passed away before the house and furniture was completed, and his widow rented the premises to Miss Belle Barlow Bush, who arranged for the completion of the furniture already underway and some additional pieces.

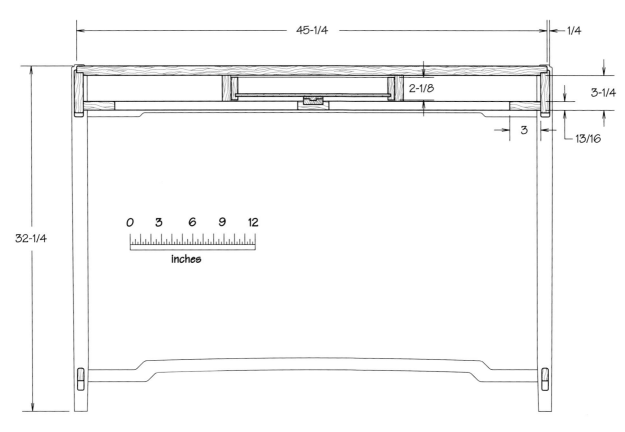

Front section

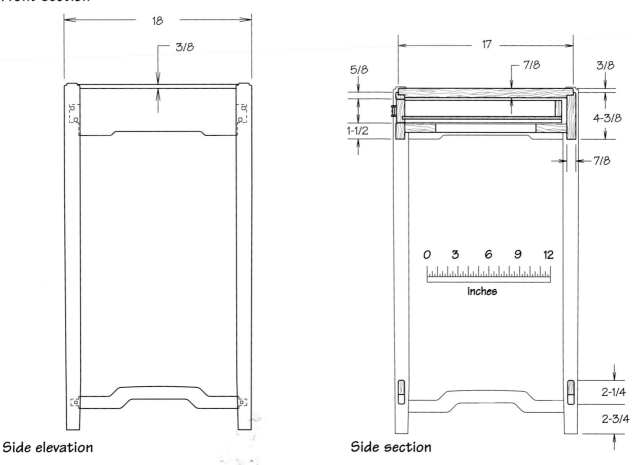

Side elevation

Side section

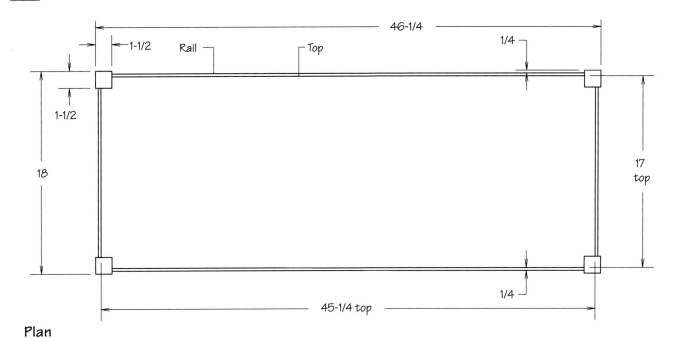

Plan

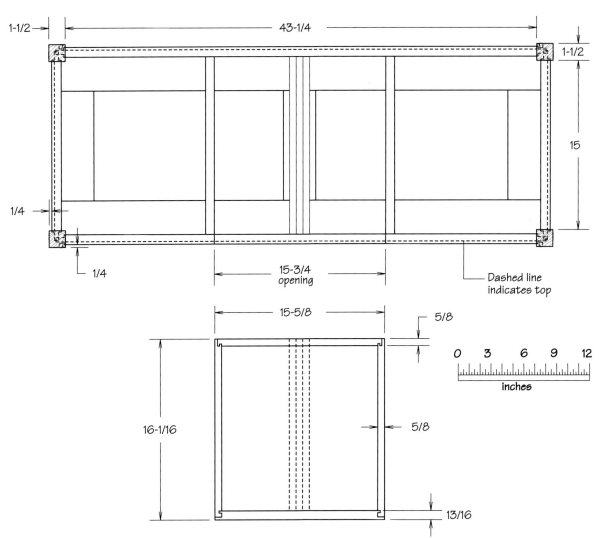

Plan section @ drawer

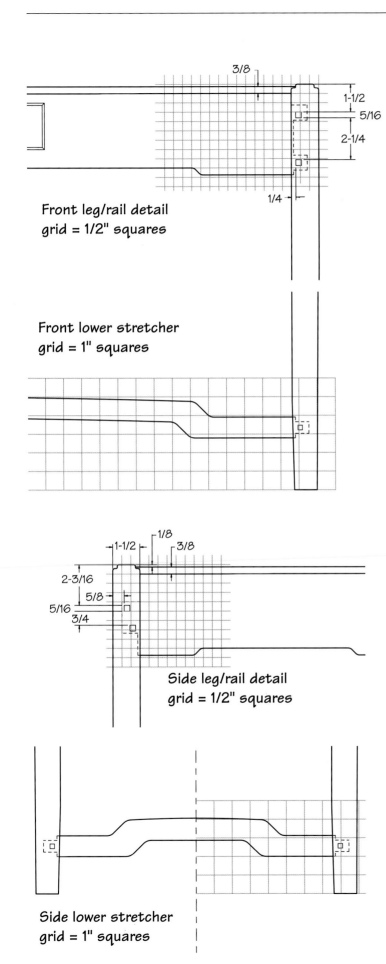

Front leg/rail detail
grid = 1/2" squares

Front lower stretcher
grid = 1" squares

Side leg/rail detail
grid = 1/2" squares

Side lower stretcher
grid = 1" squares

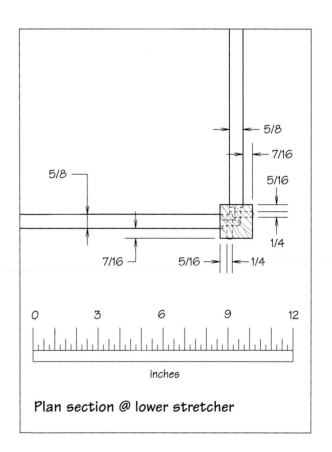

Plan section @ lower stretcher

inches

Table #1

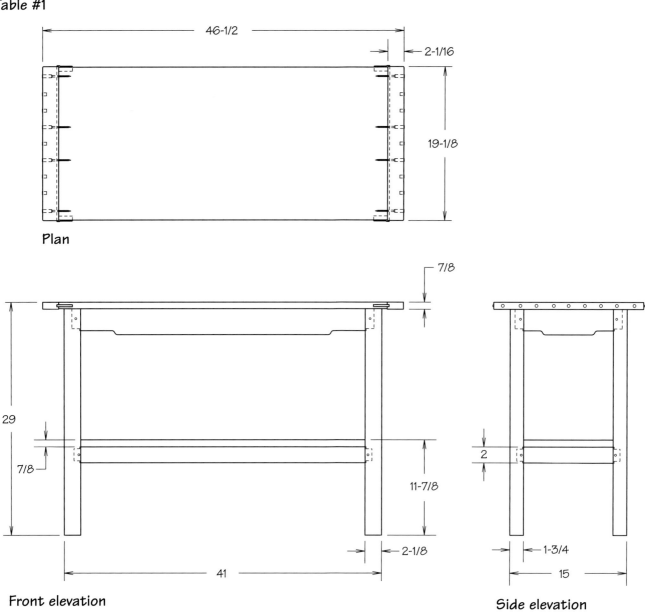

Plan

Front elevation

Side elevation

TOWNSEND OCCASIONAL TABLES

Here is a good example of the differences between the archived drawings and existing pieces. The first table is based on drawings prepared by Henry Greene in 1927 for additional furniture for the Townsend House, which was originally made for Jennie Reeve. It isn't clear whether two different tables were built, or if changes were made between the time the drawings were prepared and the table was made. This is one of the few archive drawings that shows details of the breadboard end and spline construction. These details were likely included so that someone other than the Hall brothers could recreate their details.

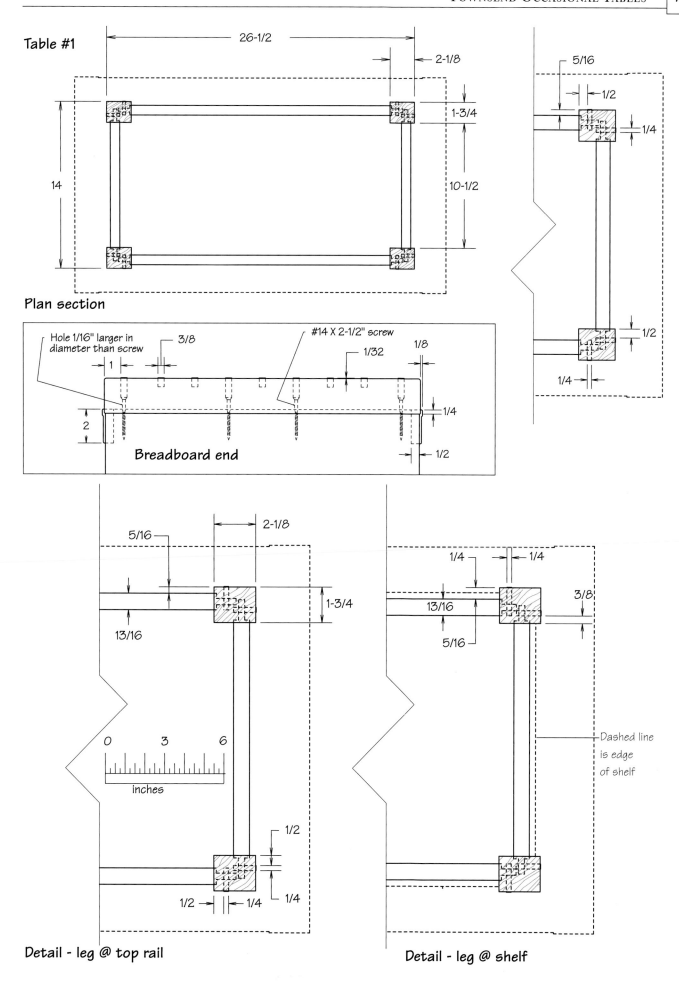

Table #1

26-1/2

2-1/8

1-3/4

14

10-1/2

5/16

1/2

1/4

1/2

1/4

Plan section

Hole 1/16" larger in diameter than screw

3/8

#14 X 2-1/2" screw

1/8

1

1/32

1/4

2

1/2

Breadboard end

5/16

2-1/8

1-3/4

13/16

0   3   6

inches

1/2

1/2   1/4   1/4

Detail - leg @ top rail

1/4   1/4

13/16

5/16

3/8

Dashed line is edge of shelf

Detail - leg @ shelf

Table #2

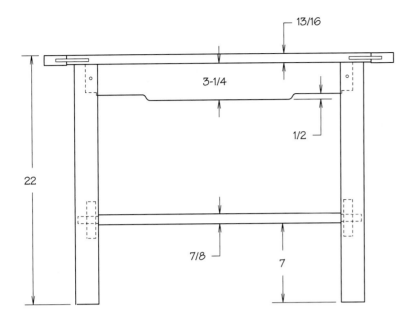

Front elevation

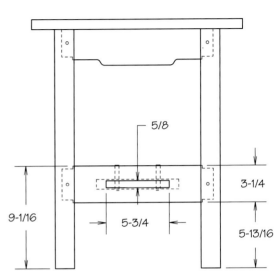

Side elevation

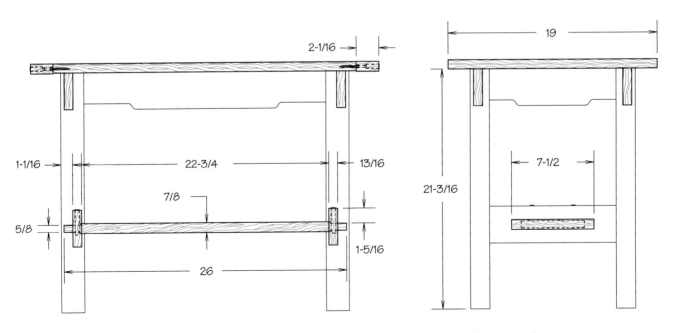

Front section

Side section

Table #2

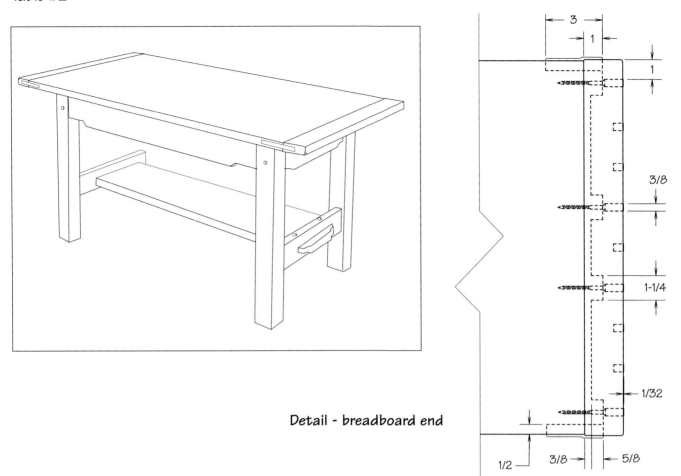

Detail - breadboard end

Plan section

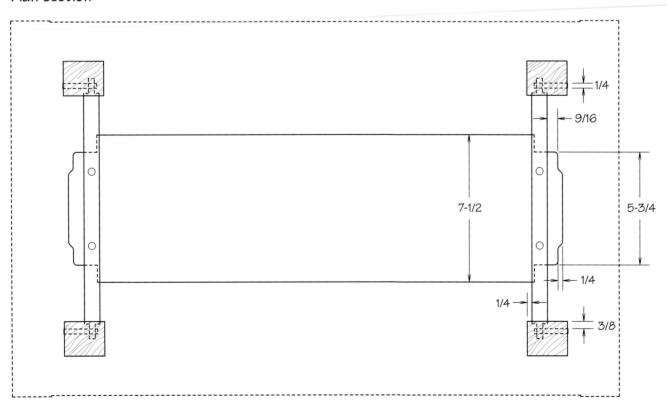

Robinson House dining table, now at the Huntington Museum, Los Angeles   *Photo: Ognan Borissov, Interfoto*

ROBINSON DINING TABLE

The furniture for the Robinson House was the first furniture to be made in the Halls' workshop, and represents the transition from the early Craftsman-influenced designs to the distinctive style of the Greene/Hall collaboration. There was also a great leap forward in the quality and attention to detail in the furniture. This table combines a base reminiscent of Japanese timber frame construction, and a top in the shape of a tsuba, a Japanese sword hilt-guard.

The Gamble House dining room table is similar in construction, and some of the details are more refined than in this example. In this table, the ebony pegs are round, and sit about $1/32$ inch proud, while in the Gamble House table, square ebony pegs were used. The extension mechanisms are also similar, but the simple shapes of the tongues and grooves become sculptural curves in the later table.

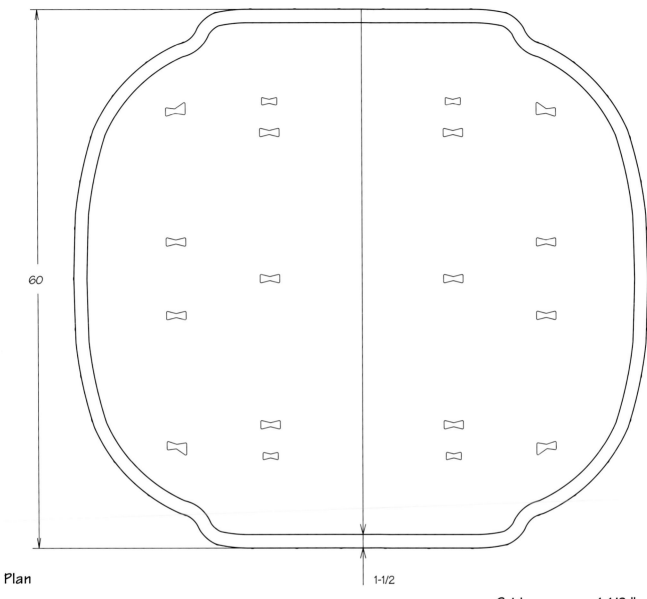

60

Plan

1-1/2

Grid squares = 1-1/2 "

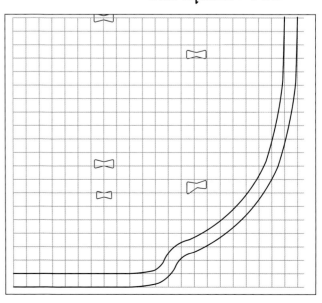

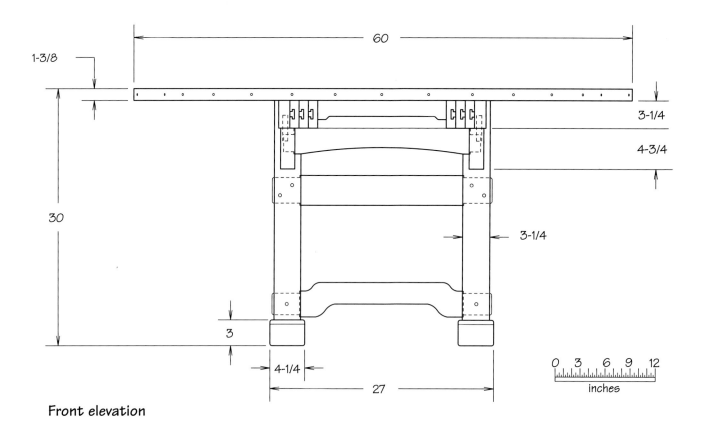

Front elevation

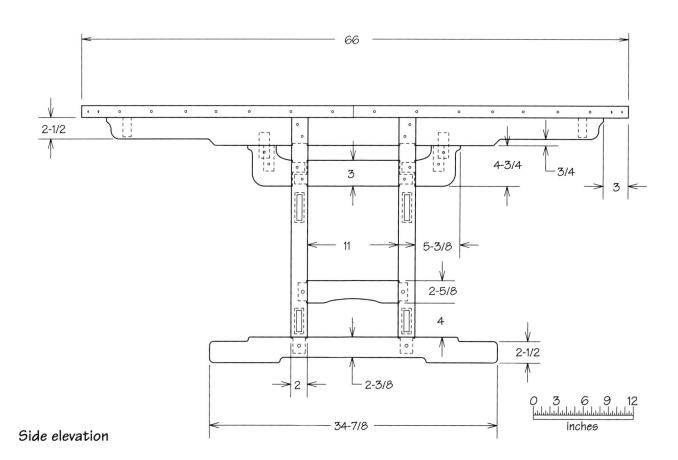

Side elevation

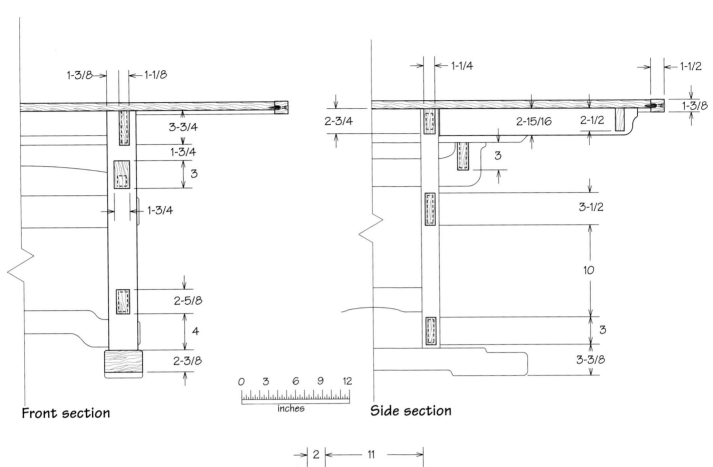

Front section

Side section

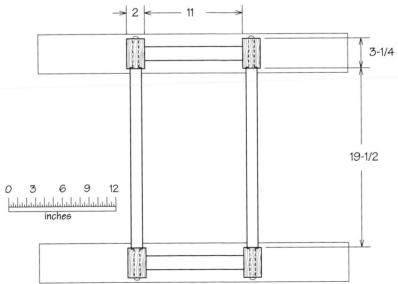

Plan section

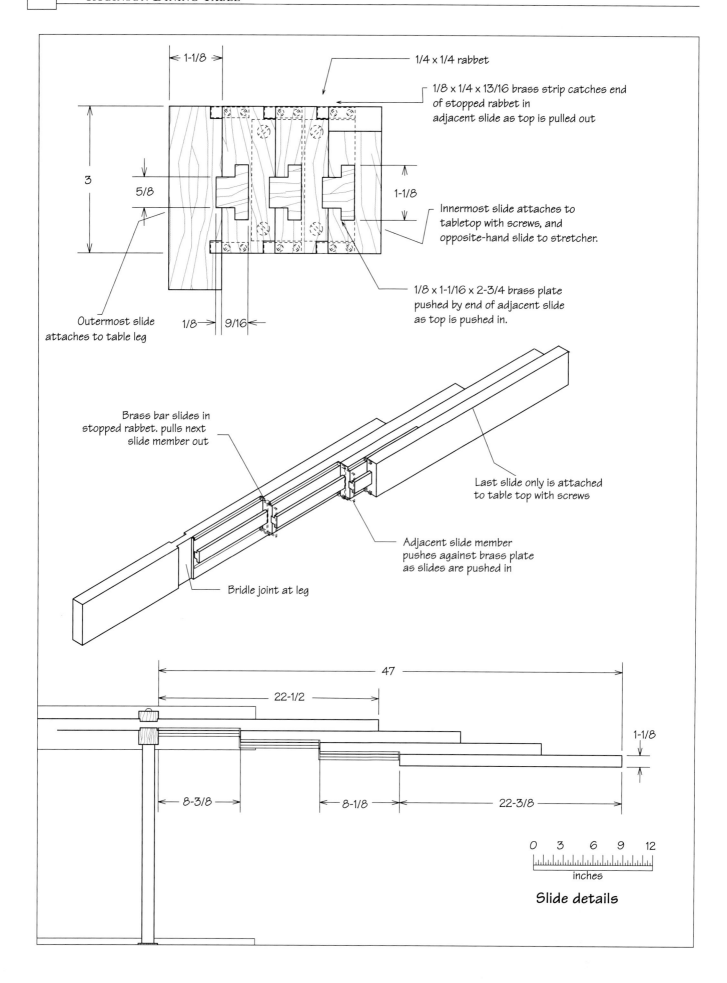

1-1/8

1/4 x 1/4 rabbet

1/8 x 1/4 x 13/16 brass strip catches end
of stopped rabbet in
adjacent slide as top is pulled out

3

5/8

1-1/8

Innermost slide attaches to
tabletop with screws, and
opposite-hand slide to stretcher.

Outermost slide
attaches to table leg

1/8   9/16

1/8 x 1-1/16 x 2-3/4 brass plate
pushed by end of adjacent slide
as top is pushed in.

Brass bar slides in
stopped rabbet. pulls next
slide member out

Last slide only is attached
to table top with screws

Adjacent slide member
pushes against brass plate
as slides are pushed in

Bridle joint at leg

47

22-1/2

1-1/8

8-3/8   8-1/8   22-3/8

0   3   6   9   12

inches

Slide details

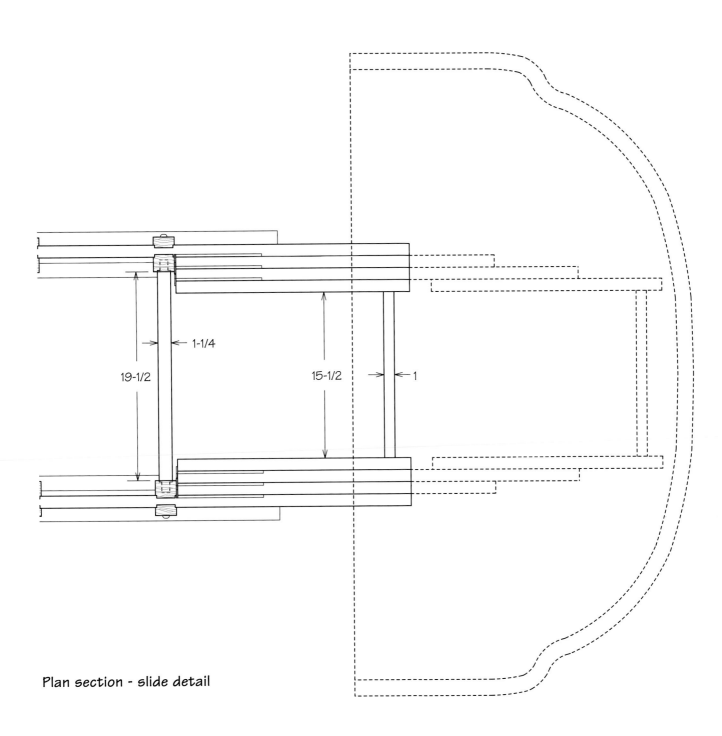

Plan section - slide detail

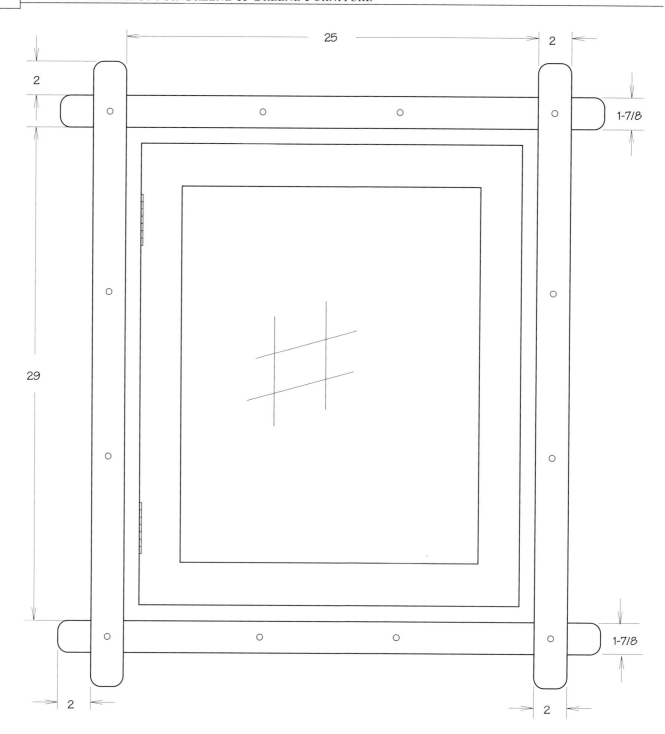

BLACKER MEDICINE CABINET

This was the typical bathroom medicine cabinet in each of the three bedrooms of the Blacker House. There were variations in height and width in the different rooms, and differences in finish. Both a painted white finish and a stained mahogany finish were used. The varying levels of the frame stiles and rails, and the extended jambs that form the frame around the door, make this an interesting cabinet.

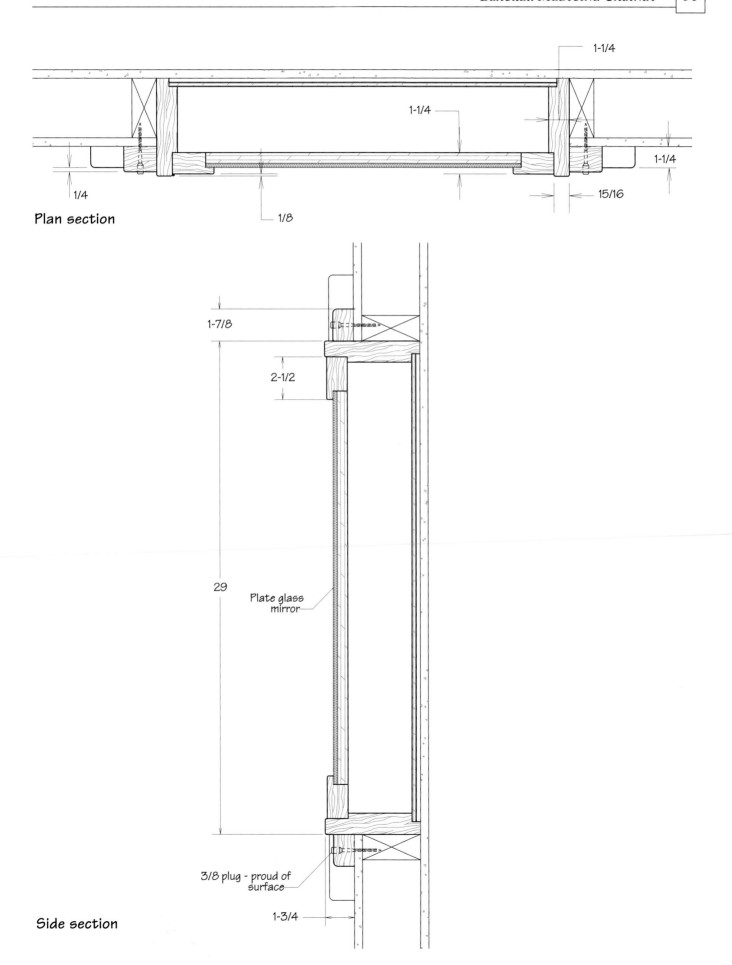

1-1/4

1-1/4

1-1/4

1/4

15/16

1/8

Plan section

1-7/8

2-1/2

29

Plate glass
mirror

3/8 plug - proud of
surface

1-3/4

Side section

Gamble House mirror

Photo: Ognan Borissov, Interfoto

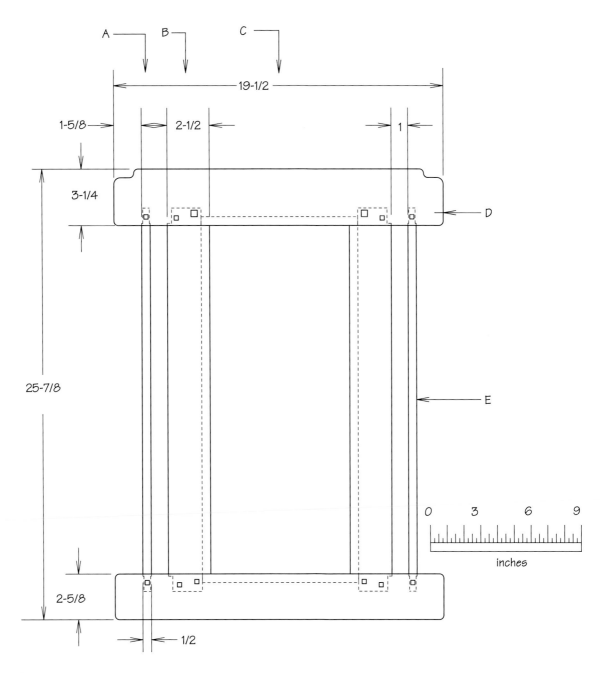

Front elevation

GAMBLE MIRROR

There were several mirror and picture frames made for specific locations in the Gamble House, each one a little different. The one I have chosen to draw has especially nice proportions, and would make a good piece for practice joints,

finishes, and plug techniques without using a lot of material. The one shown in the photo at left is equally handsome, and features a novel hanging system that could work in any interior with a picture rail.

Side sections

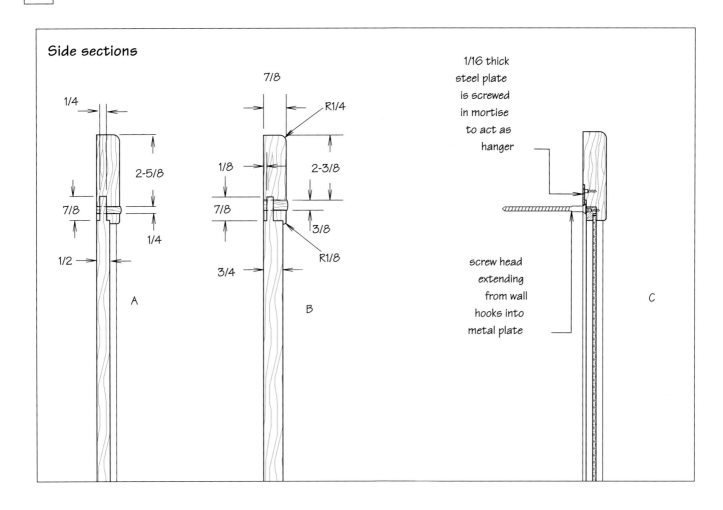

1/16 thick steel plate is screwed in mortise to act as hanger

screw head extending from wall hooks into metal plate

Plan sections

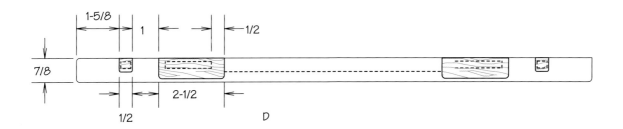

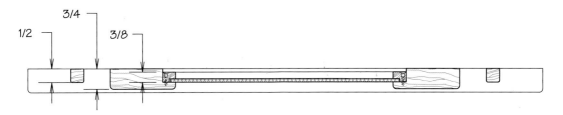

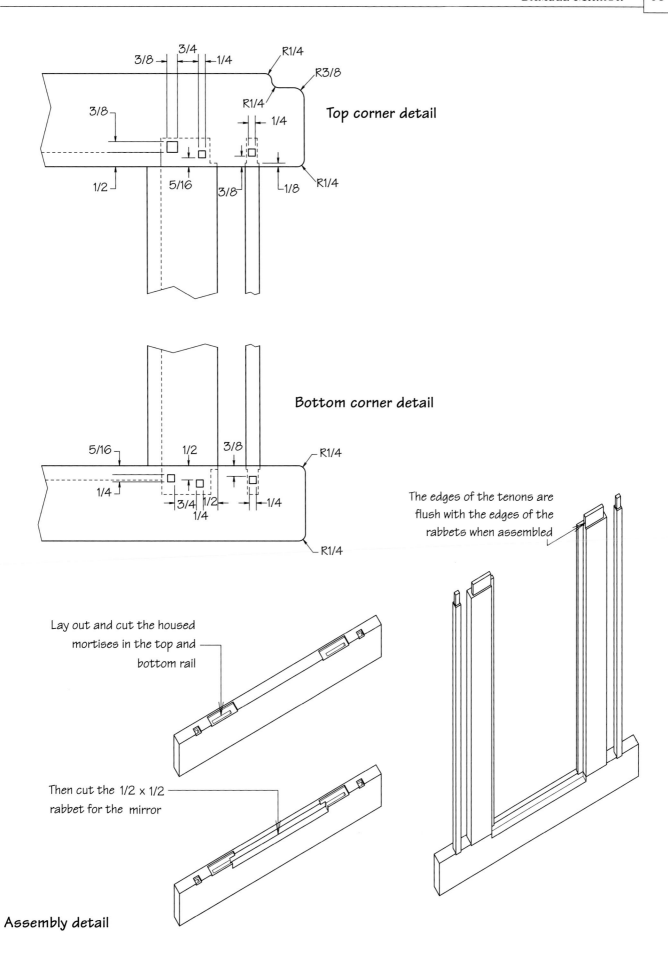

Top corner detail

Bottom corner detail

The edges of the tenons are flush with the edges of the rabbets when assembled

Lay out and cut the housed mortises in the top and bottom rail

Then cut the 1/2 x 1/2 rabbet for the mirror

Assembly detail

TICHENOR BEDROOM CHEST

This bedroom chest was one of the last pieces of furniture made before the association of the Greenes and the Halls. Cloud lift patterns appear in the handles and in the rails of the panels, but the shaping and rounding of the curves is not as refined as in the work of the Halls. The round pegs are proud about $1/8$ inch, much further than the $1/32$ inch to $1/16$ inch projection that was used in later pieces. The joints in the drawers are half-blind dovetails, indicating that the rabbetted tongue and groove joint came into use when the furniture began to be produced by the Hall brothers.

This is a nice, well-made piece of furniture, but not made at the same level of the later pieces. It isn't known who made the Tichenor furniture; there are three or four shops that could have built it, but no direct evidence. The design vocabulary of the Greenes was starting to blossom, but whoever made this piece didn't quite understand the language.

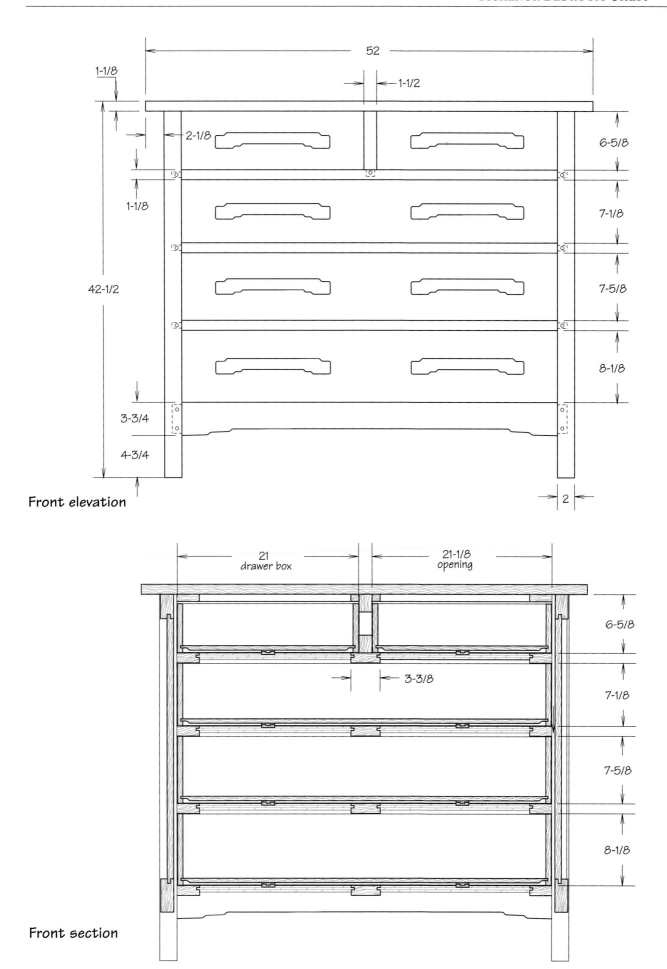

Front elevation

Front section

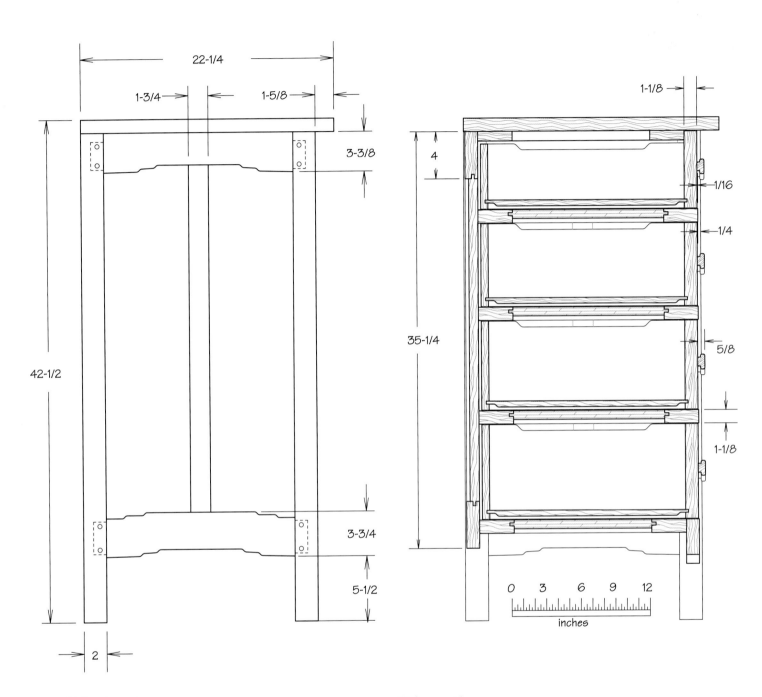

Side elevation

Side section

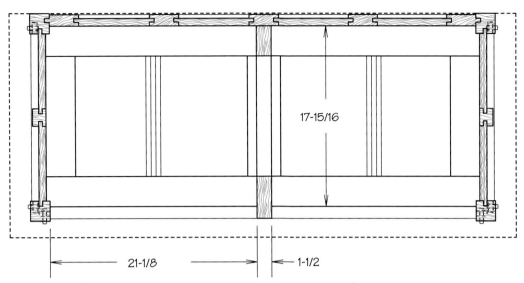

Plan section @ top above drawers

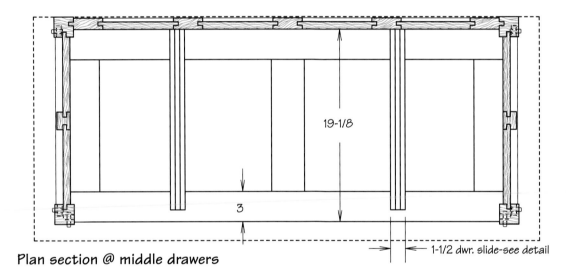

Plan section @ middle drawers

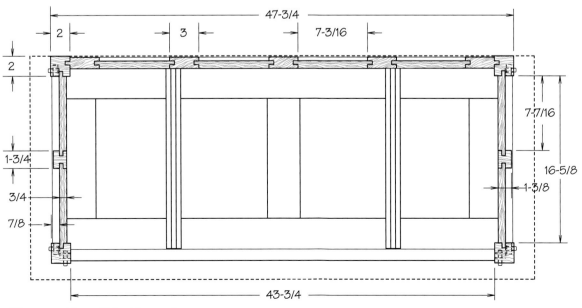

Plan section @ bottom drawer

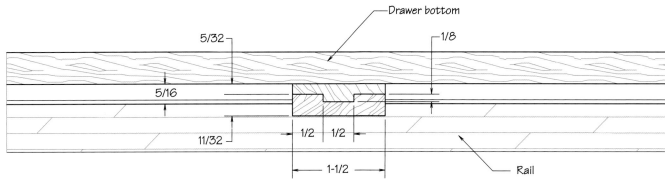

Drawer bottom

5/32

1/8

5/16

11/32

1/2 1/2

1-1/2

Rail

Drawer slide detail

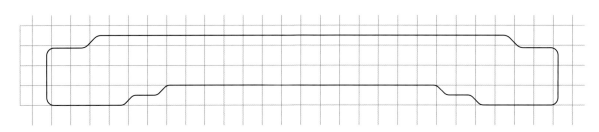

Handle detail grid = 1/2" squares

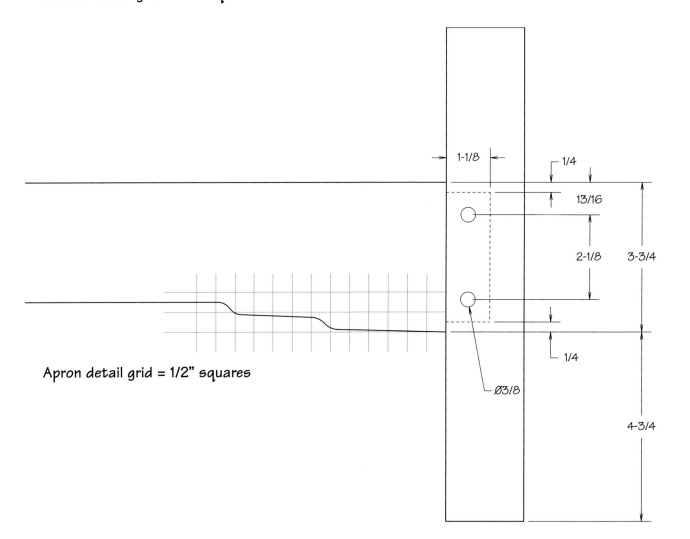

1-1/8

1/4

13/16

2-1/8

3-3/4

1/4

Ø3/8

4-3/4

Apron detail grid = 1/2" squares

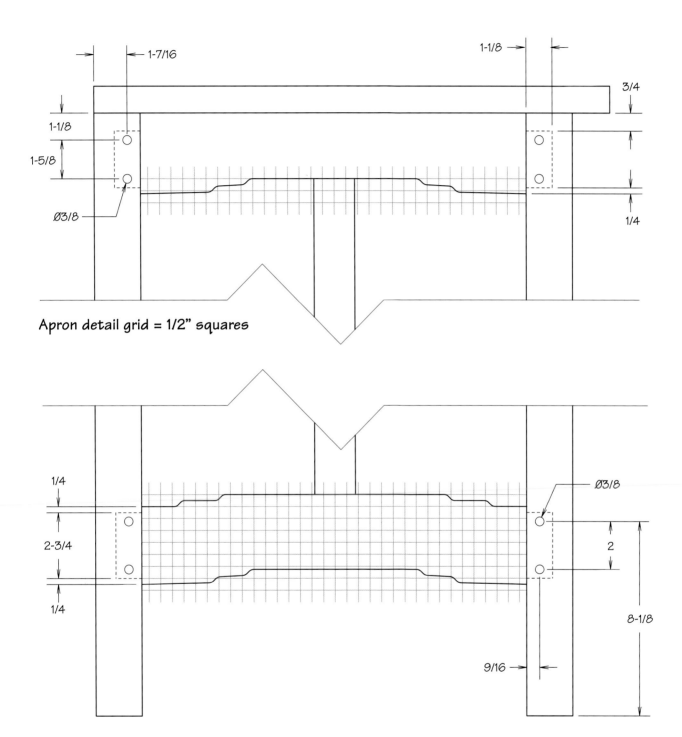

Apron detail grid = 1/2" squares

Rail detail grid = 1/2" squares

BUSH CURIO CABINET

Designed to live on top of the hall table, this small curio was designed to hold some special items treasured by Miss Bush. The cut-out area in the shelves on the right was to accommodate one of these pieces. The original drawings showed two layouts for the leaded glass on the doors, both more intricate than what was eventually made.

The blocks holding the bail handles, as well as the inlays on the lower rail of the doors are ebony. It is amazing how much effort and detail is contained in this diminutive piece.

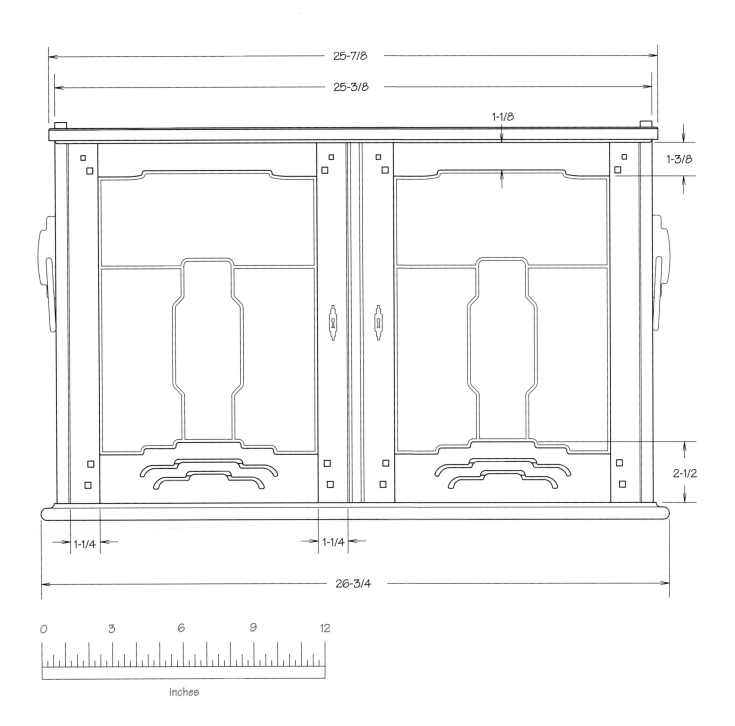

25-7/8

25-3/8

1-1/8

1-3/8

2-1/2

1-1/4

1-1/4

26-3/4

0   3   6   9   12

inches

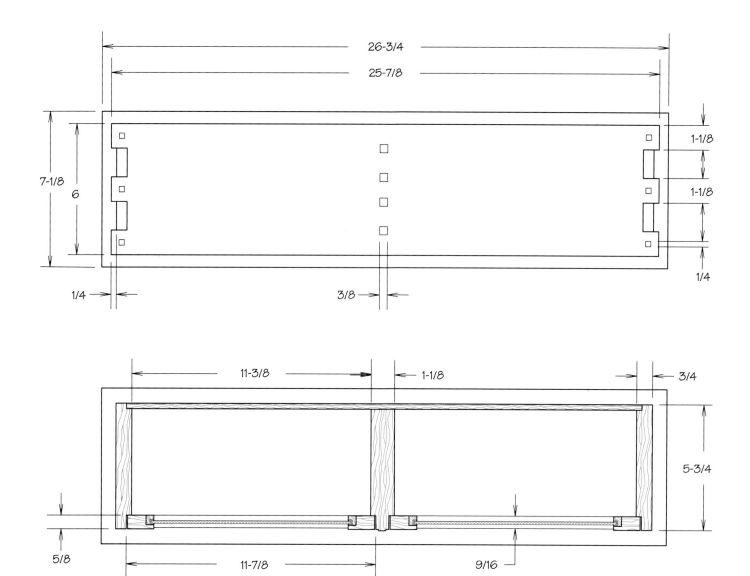

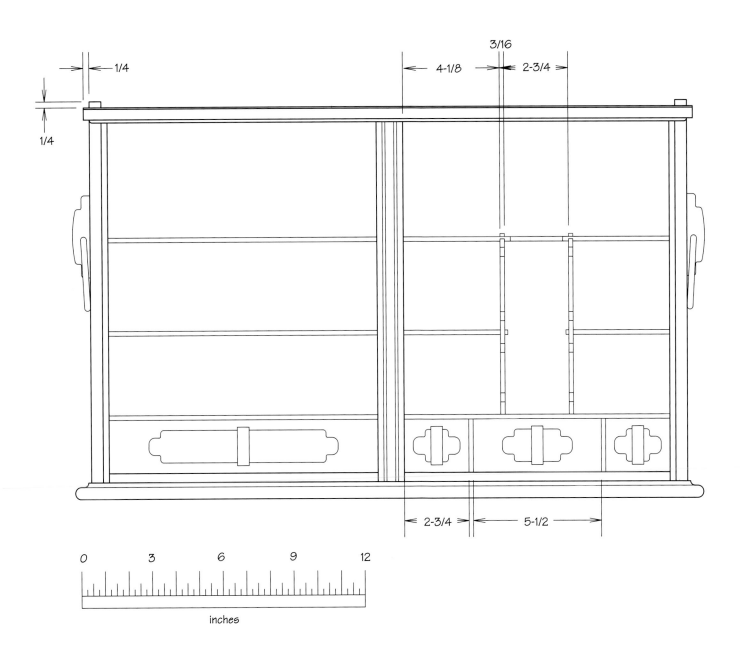

inches

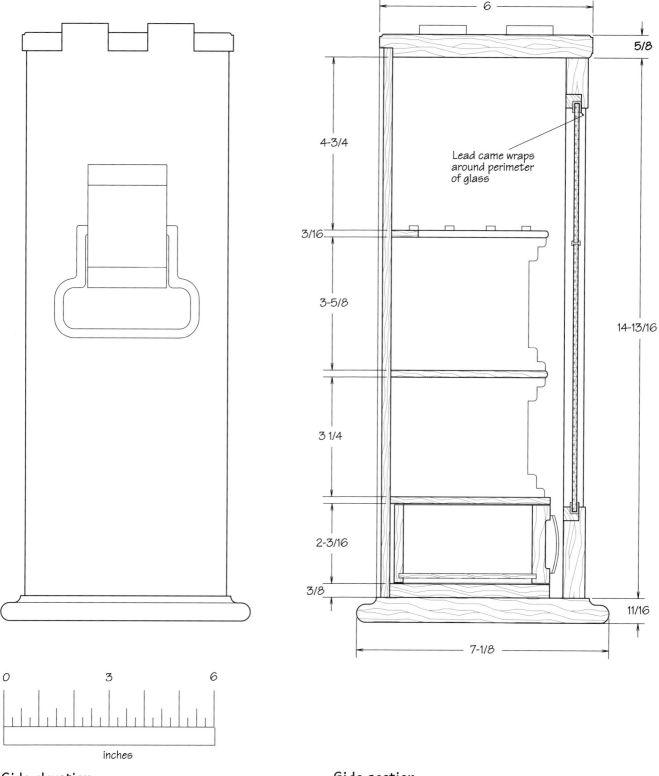

Lead came wraps
around perimeter
of glass

6

5/8

4-3/4

3/16

3-5/8

3 1/4

14-13/16

2-3/16

3/8

11/16

7-1/8

0   3   6

inches

Side elevation

Side section

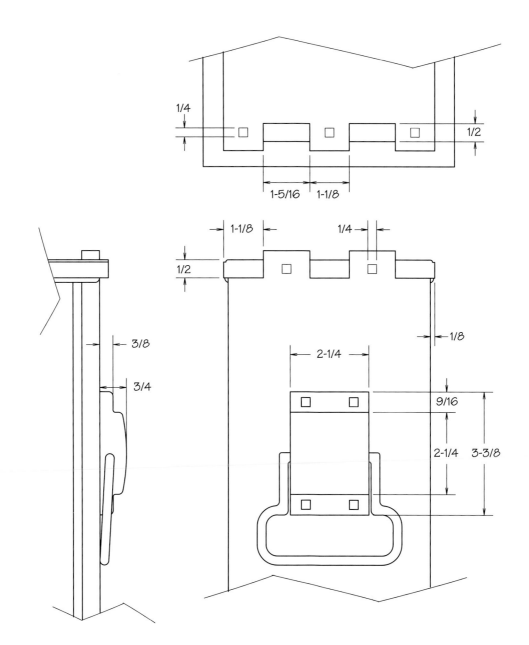

Details at top corner

inches

Gamble House bed

Photo: Ognan Borissov, Interfoto

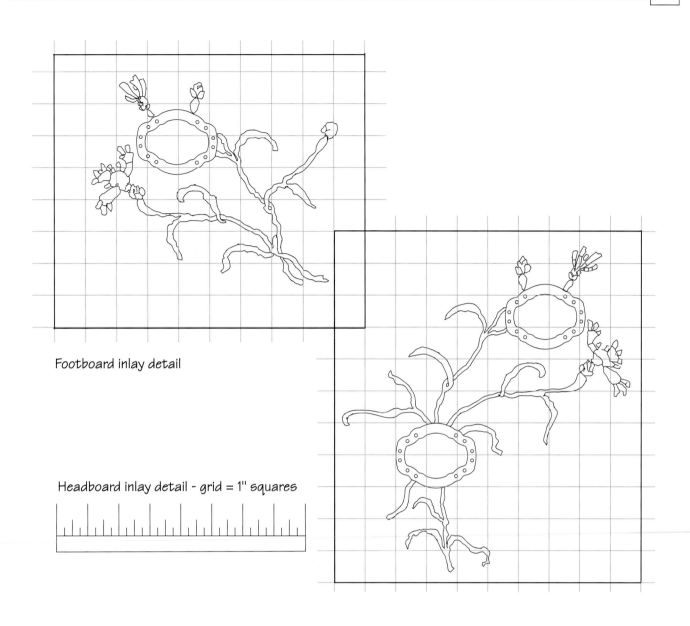

Footboard inlay detail

Headboard inlay detail - grid = 1" squares

GAMBLE BED

One of the matching pieces of the black walnut master bedroom set is a pair of twin beds, a fashionable sleeping arrangement of the day. I've taken the liberty to follow the drawings of the original size with an adaptation to a modern queen-size.

The inlays are similar to those on the other pieces, the branches are realistically carved and are proud of the surrounding surface. The flowers are semi-precious stones - lapis, jade and mother of pearl. The tsuba shapes are open in their centers, and are made of ebony with small brass pins. In addition to being an example of highly skilled workmanship, these beds also show the lengths that the Halls would go to in including details in unlikely places. One might not expect the inlay to be on both sides of the footboards, but it is. The real surprise is that it is rendered on both sides of the headboards as well.

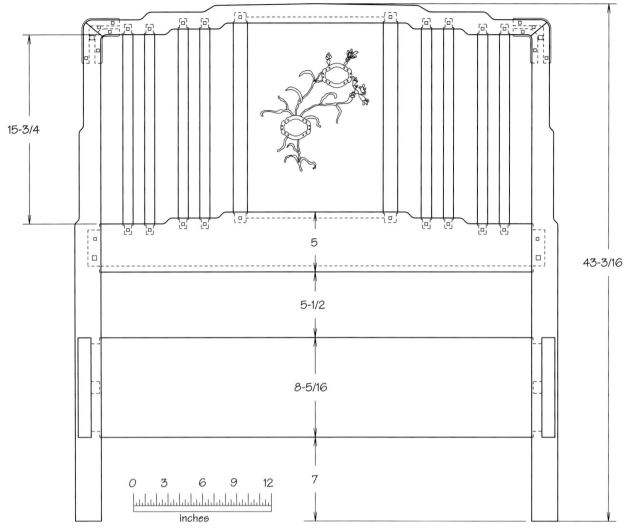

15-3/4

43-3/16

5

5-1/2

8-5/16

7

0   3   6   9   12

inches

Headboard elevation

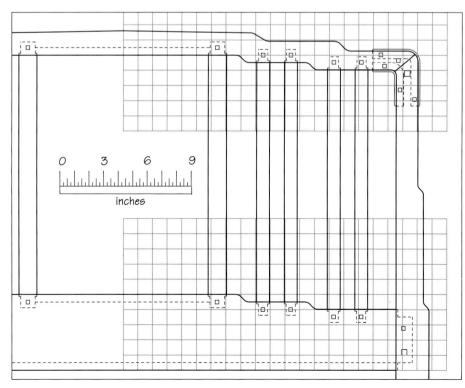

0   3   6   9

inches

Grid = 1" squares

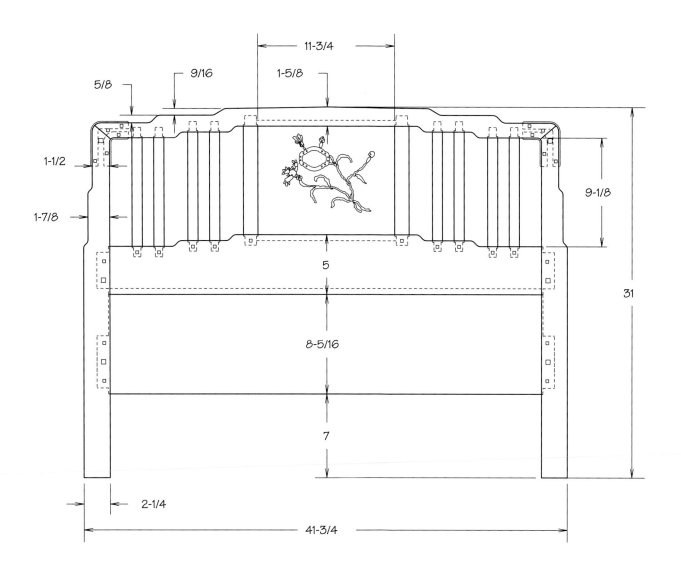

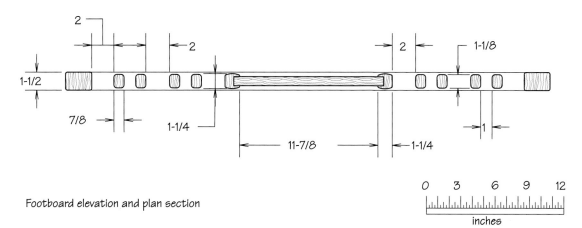

Footboard elevation and plan section

0 3 6 9 12

inches

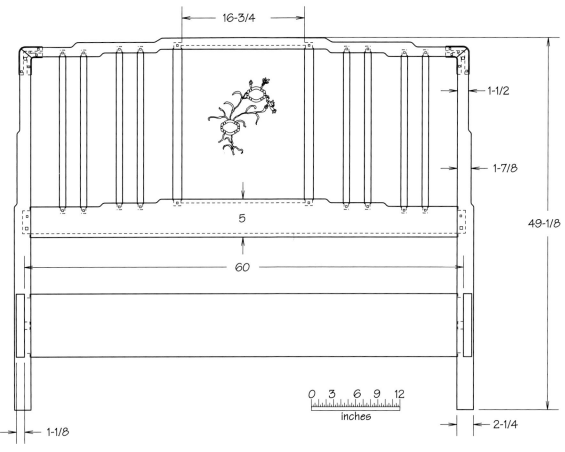

Queen-size headboard - elevation

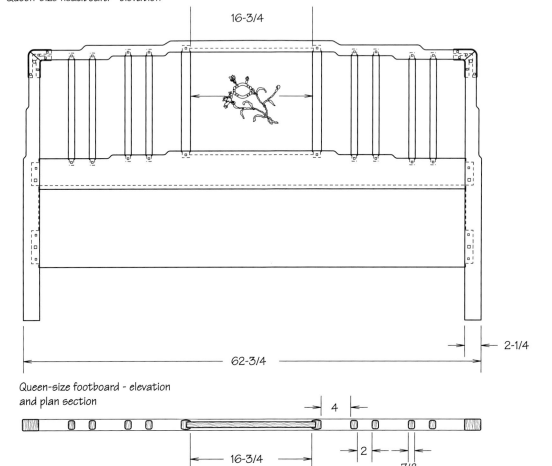

Queen-size footboard - elevation
and plan section

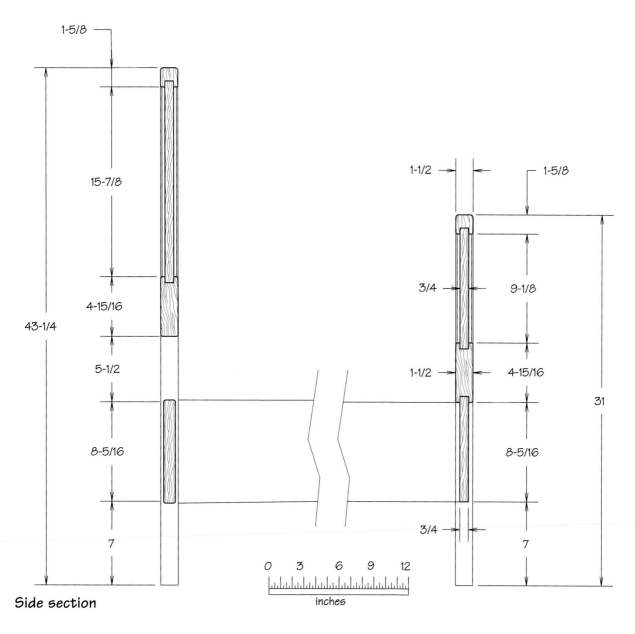

1-5/8

15-7/8

43-1/4

4-15/16

5-1/2

8-5/16

7

Side section

0   3   6   9   12

inches

1-1/2

1-5/8

3/4

9-1/8

1-1/2

4-15/16

31

8-5/16

3/4

7

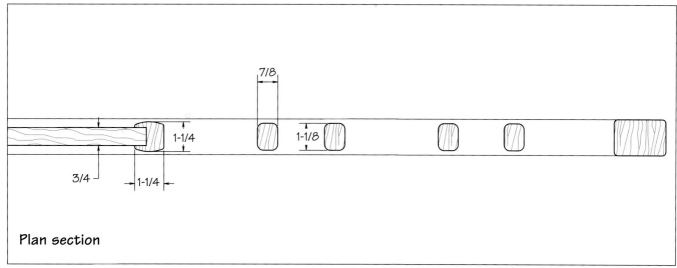

7/8

1-1/4

1-1/8

3/4

1-1/4

Plan section

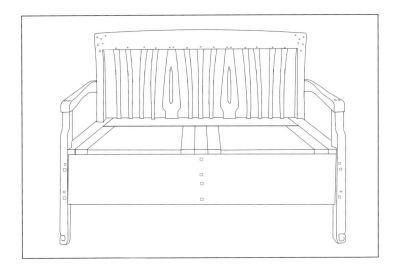

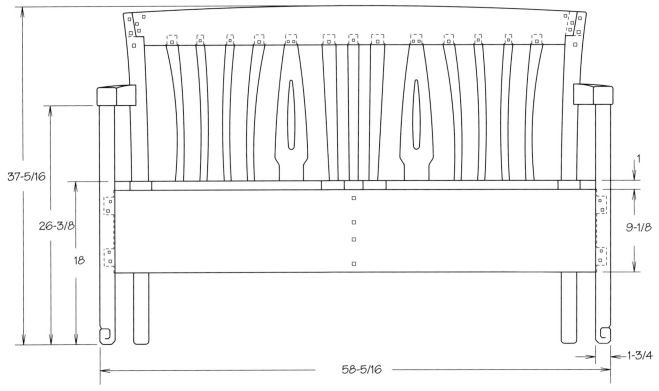

Front elevation

BLACKER HALL SEAT

This bench with storage below the seats was made for the entry hall, and has many features in common with the Blacker House chairs, although the construction is simpler. The legs are rectangular, and the rail at the top of the back isn't curved in plan.

This form of bench was typical in the Arts & Crafts period, and is a practical and popular form. The seats are hinged, lifting up to give access to storage space below.

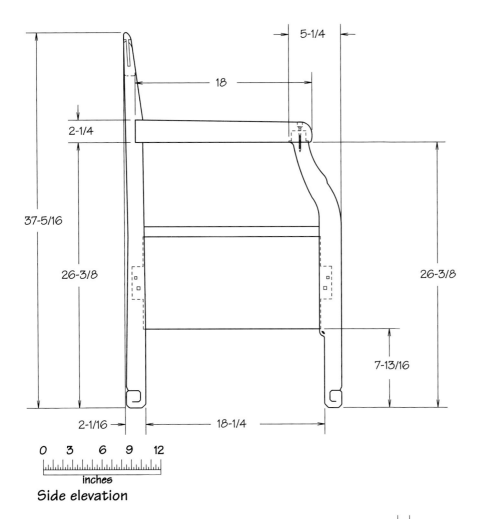

5-1/4

18

2-1/4

37-5/16

26-3/8

26-3/8

7-13/16

2-1/16

18-1/4

0   3   6   9   12

inches

Side elevation

1-1/4

4-5/16

15   1/2

7/8

1

9-1/8   7-5/8

18

21-1/16

Side section

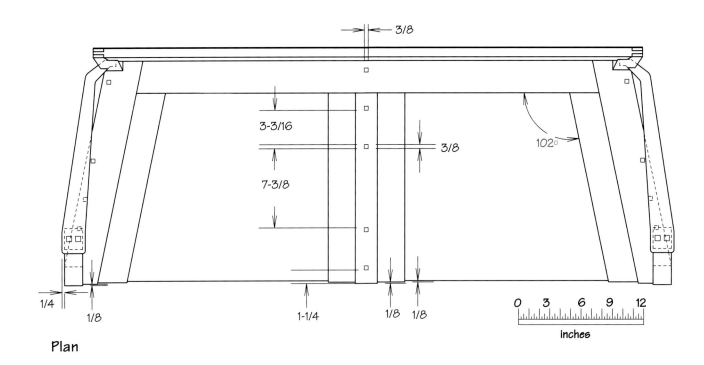

Plan

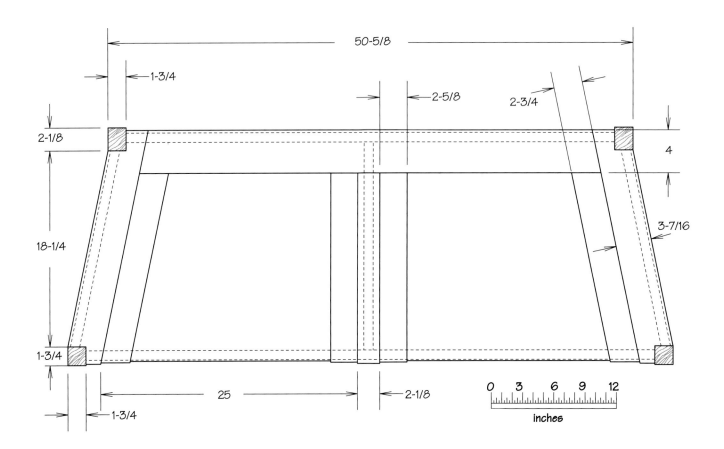

Plan section below seat

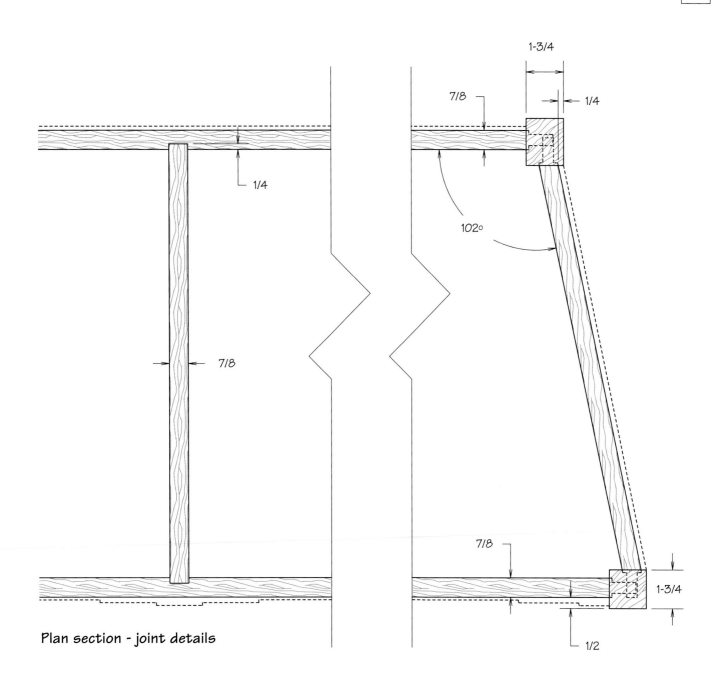

1-3/4

7/8

1/4

1/4

102°

7/8

7/8

1-3/4

1/2

Plan section - joint details

Leg and arm detail
grid = 1" squares

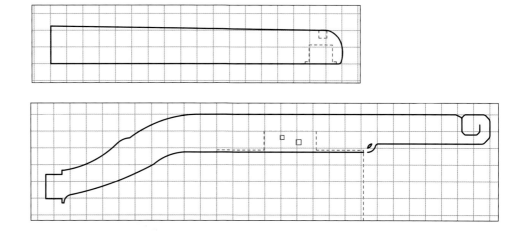

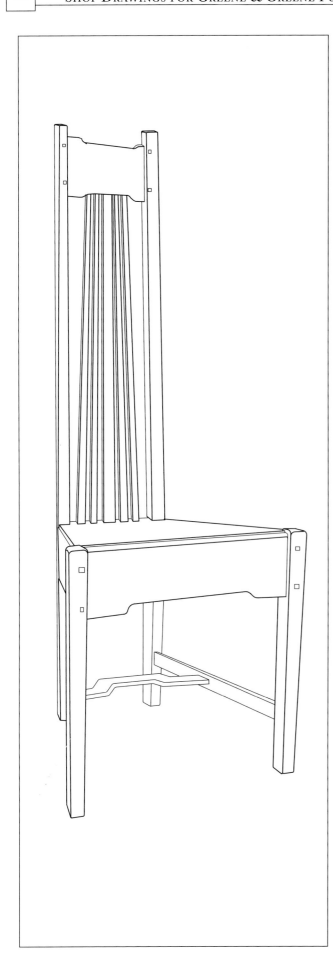

BOLTON HALL CHAIR

High-backed chairs first appeared in the early 20th century in the designs of Charles Rennie Mackintosh and Frank Lloyd Wright. This rendition by the Greenes has their signature design elements of cloud lifts and ebony pegs. Although it would make a great dining room chair, only two of these chairs were made to flank the table in the entry hall. There are some curious elements that make this chair a challenge to build.

One is the shape of the legs: the parallelogram shape instead of rectangular increases the difficulty in making the joints, and this was a feature of several Greene and Greene chairs. The way the seat is enclosed by the rails, and the number of glue blocks below, makes this risky construction. The chair on display at the Huntington Museum has a small crack in the front of the seat because of seasonal wood movement. I would be very careful in choosing wood for the seat, and would eliminate the cross grain braces below. Depending on the season, I would leave more of a gap between the seat and rails than is shown in the drawings.

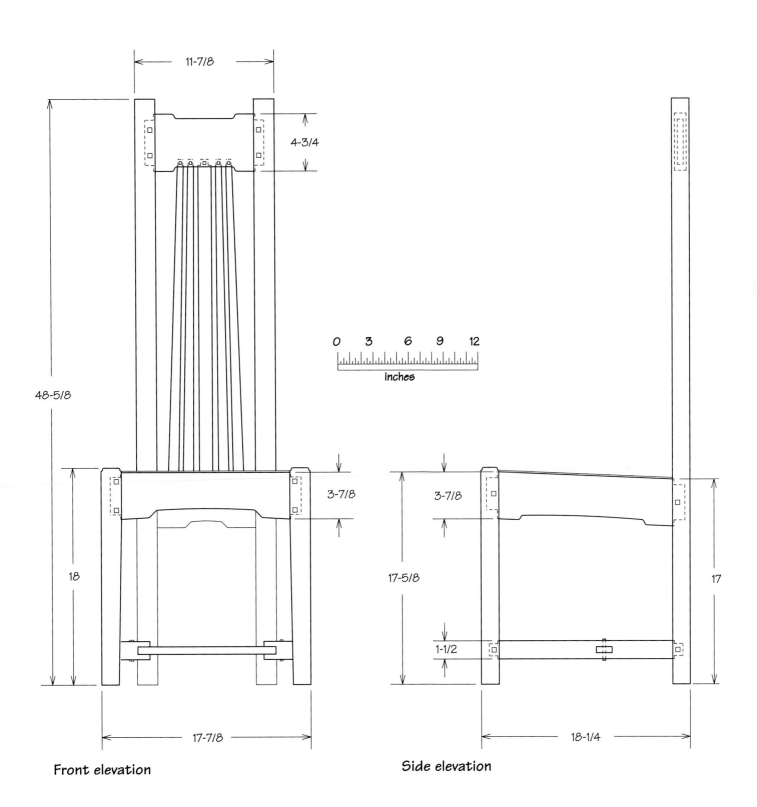

11-7/8

4-3/4

48-5/8

0   3   6   9   12
inches

3-7/8

3-7/8

18

17-5/8

17

1-1/2

17-7/8

18-1/4

Front elevation

Side elevation

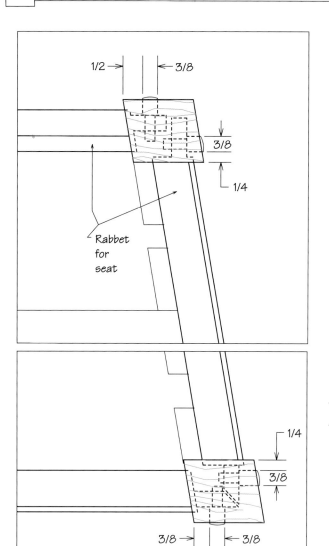

1/2   3/8

3/8

1/4

Rabbet
for
seat

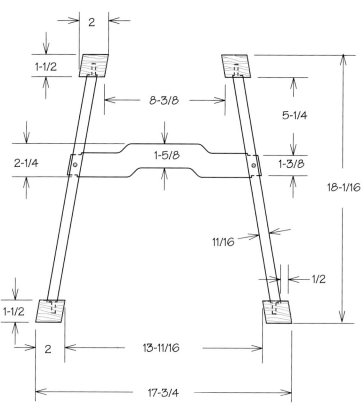

2

1-1/2

8-3/8

5-1/4

2-1/4   1-5/8   1-3/8

18-1/16

11/16

1/2

1-1/2

2   13-11/16

17-3/4

Plan section at lower stretcher

1/4

3/8

3/8   3/8

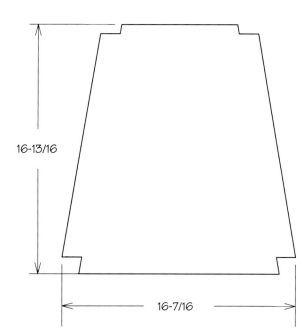

16-13/16

16-7/16

Seat plan

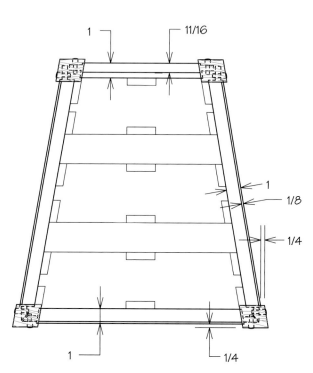

1   11/16

1

1/8

1/4

1

1/4

Plan section below seat

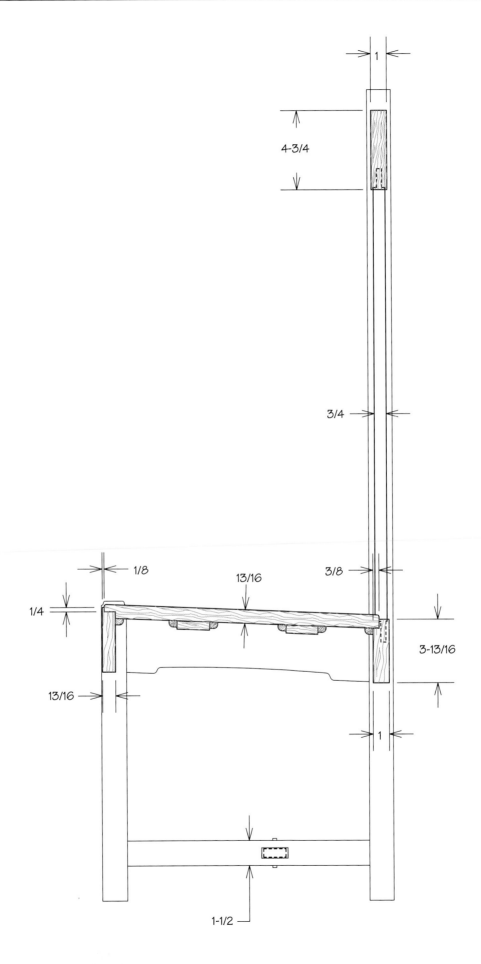

1

4-3/4

3/4

1/8

13/16

3/8

1/4

3-13/16

13/16

1

1-1/2

Side section

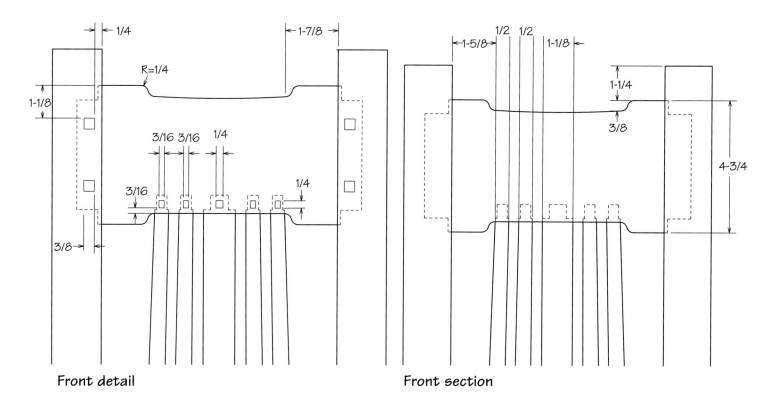

Front detail

Front section

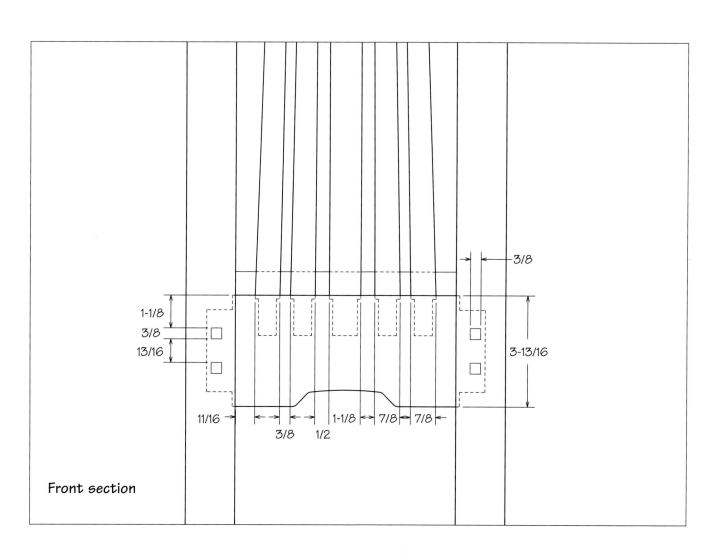

Front section

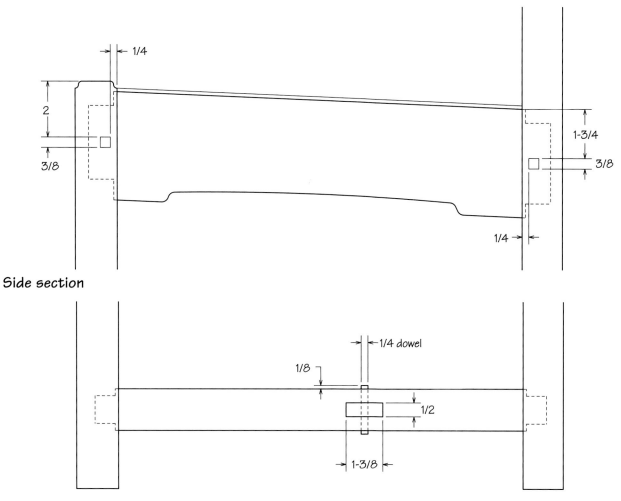

Side section

1/4

2

3/8

1-3/4

3/8

1/4

Side section

1/4 dowel

1/8

1/2

1-3/8

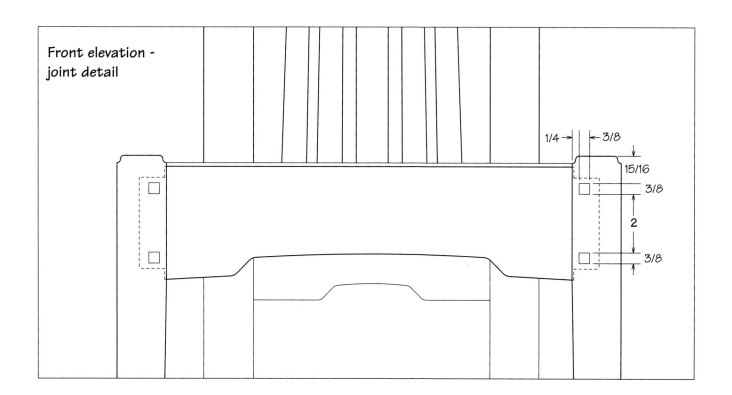

Front elevation -
joint detail

1/4

3/8

15/16

3/8

2

3/8

Robinson House side chair, now at the Huntington Museum, Los Angeles   *Photo: Ognan Borissov, Interfoto*

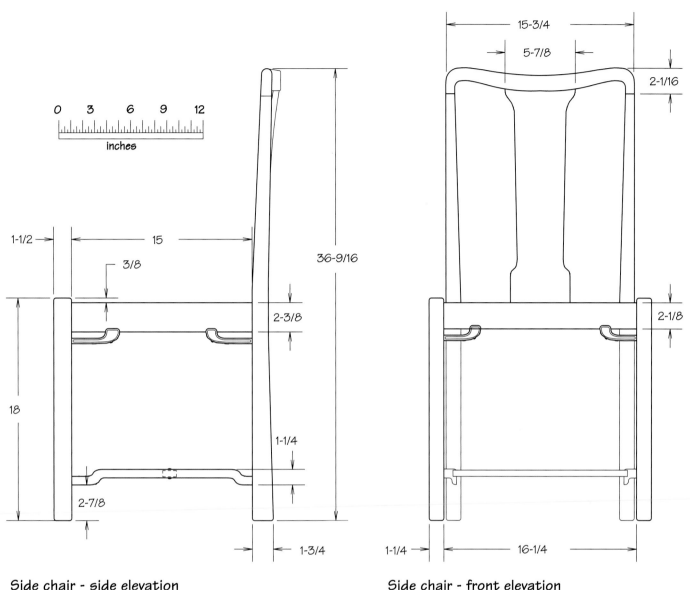

0   3   6   9   12
inches

Side chair - side elevation

Side chair - front elevation

ROBINSON CHAIR

The dining room chairs for the Robinson house mark the maturation of the Greene Brothers style. Influenced more by classical Oriental design than by Arts & Crafts designs, they are a departure from their previous furniture work, and an indication of the more stylized chairs in the Gamble, Blacker and Freeman Ford Houses.

The seat is an upholstered slip seat, and the inside corners at the intersection of the legs and cross rails should be reinforced with 45-degree blocks, which are also used for attaching the base of the slip seat. The side chair is shown here, the arm chair appears on page 125.

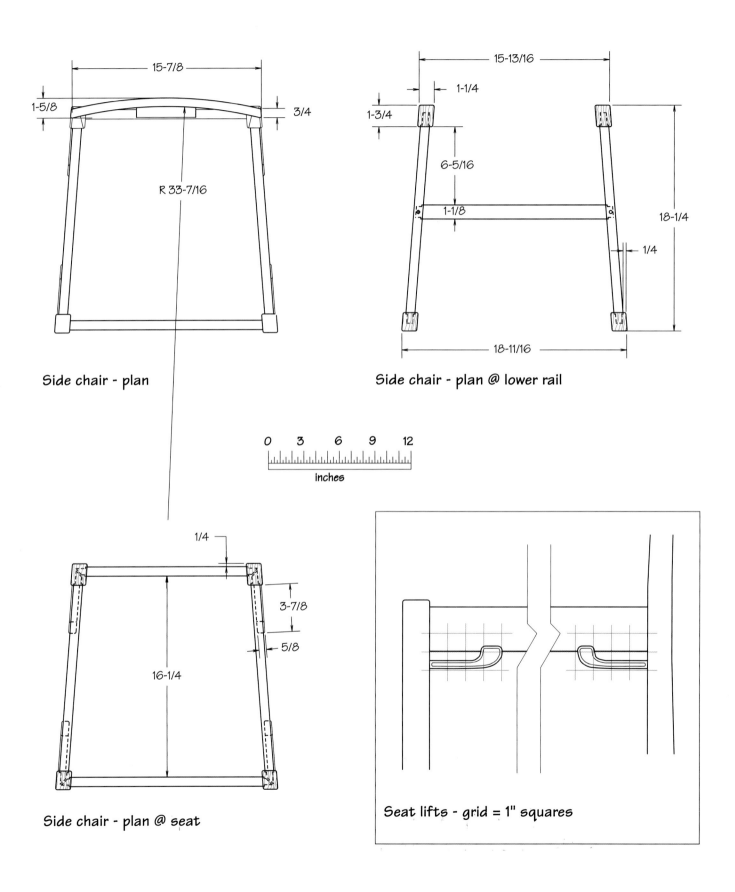

Side chair - plan

Side chair - plan @ lower rail

Side chair - plan @ seat

Seat lifts - grid = 1" squares

15-7/8

1-5/8

3/4

R 33-7/16

15-13/16

1-1/4

1-3/4

6-5/16

1-1/8

18-1/4

1/4

18-11/16

0   3   6   9   12

inches

1/4

3-7/8

5/8

16-1/4

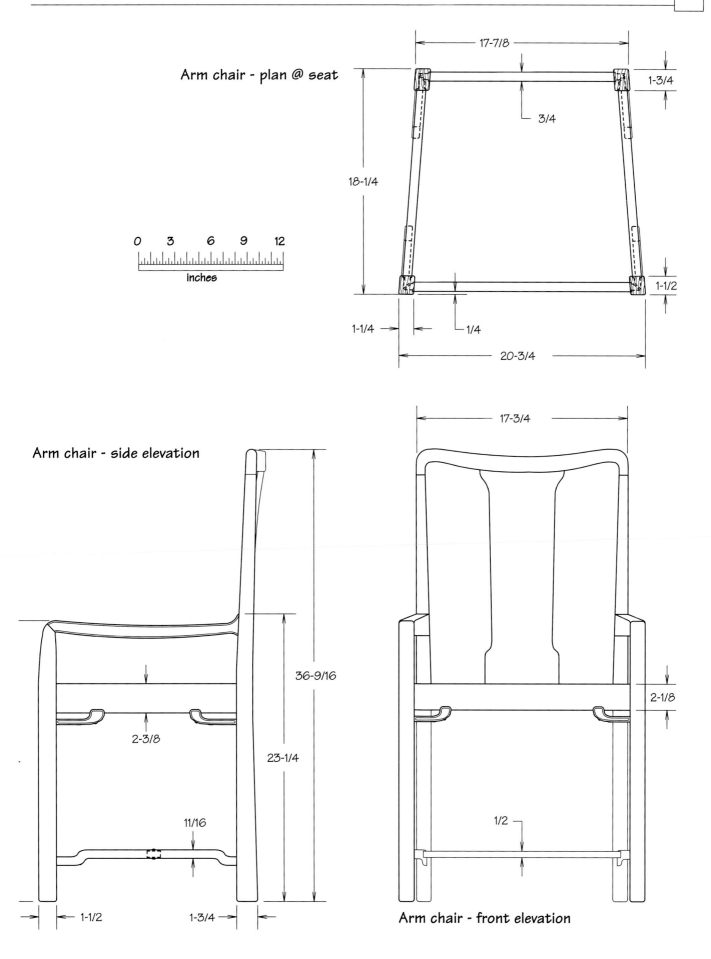

Arm chair - plan @ seat

17-7/8

1-3/4

3/4

18-1/4

1-1/2

1-1/4   1/4

20-3/4

0   3   6   9   12

inches

Arm chair - side elevation

17-3/4

2-1/8

36-9/16

2-3/8

23-1/4

1/2

11/16

1-1/2   1-3/4

Arm chair - front elevation

Thorsen House plant stand, now at the Huntington Museum, Los Angeles   *Photo: Ognan Borissov, Interfoto*

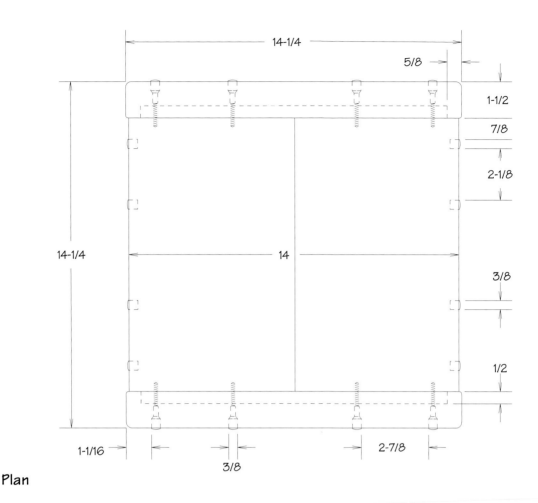

Plan

THORSEN PLANT STAND

This small stand contains many Greene and Greene design elements in a small package. The cutouts in the rails below the breadboard top are similar to the tsuba and other oriental curved shapes that were often used. The offset peg locations on the leg and rail connections indicate that the mortise and tenon joints are offset, as shown in the drawings. This is a clever solution to a common furniture engineering problem providing strong joints where two rails are mortised into a common leg. The top presents a puzzle in that there are plugs present on both the breadboard ends, and the long-grain edges. The

plugs in the breadboards are functional, those on the adjacent edges are not.

The other construction question is how to handle the intersection of the corners of the lower shelf and the legs. There is always the question of whether to notch the corners of the shelf around the legs, or to put a dado in the legs to house the corners of the shelf. With the edge of the shelf as close as it is to the outer edges of the legs, the Halls would likely have done both to hide the top of the shelf, without cutting too deeply into the leg.

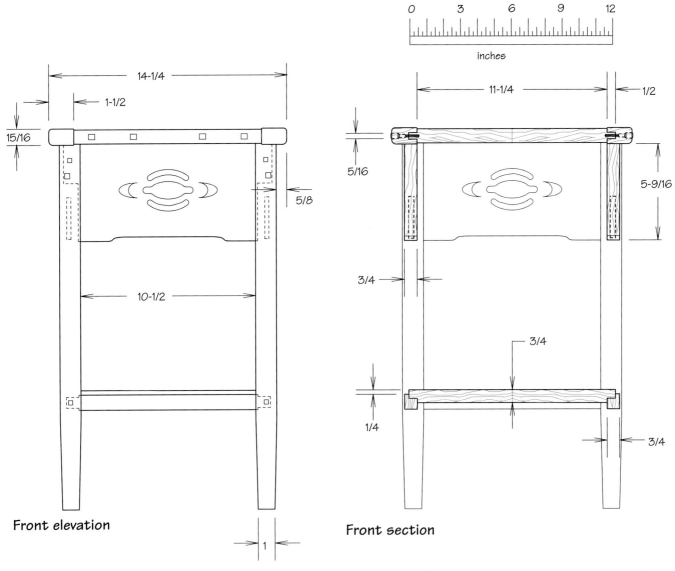

Front elevation

Front section

inches

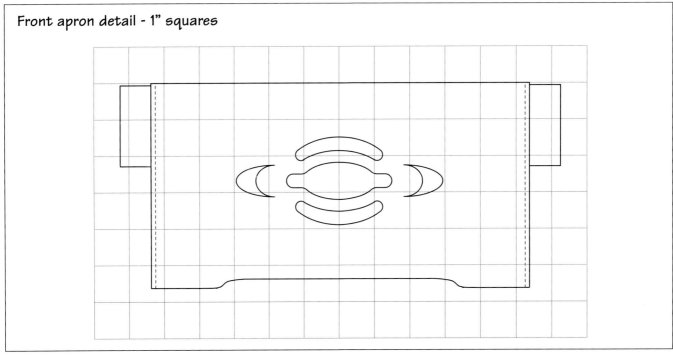

Front apron detail - 1" squares

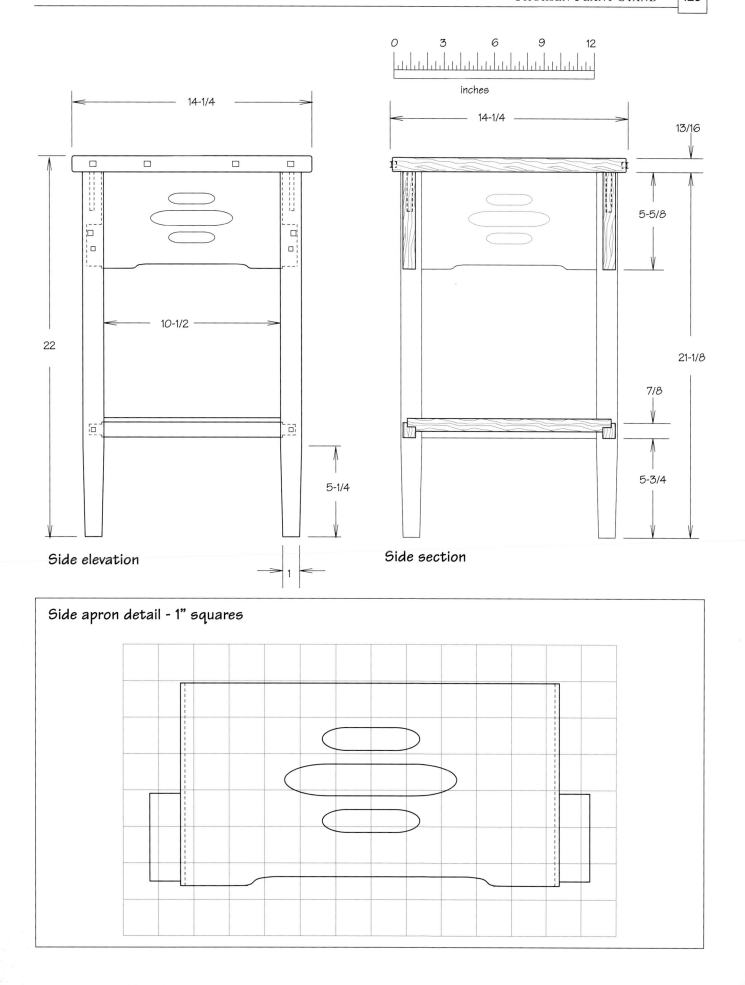

0   3   6   9   12
inches

14-1/4

14-1/4

13/16

22

10-1/2

5-5/8

21-1/8

7/8

5-1/4

5-3/4

Side elevation

1

Side section

Side apron detail - 1" squares

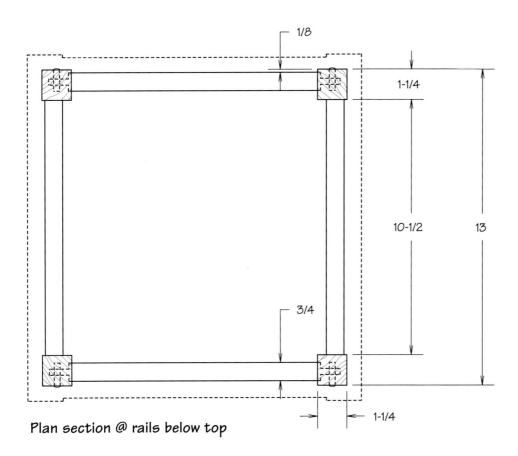

Plan section @ rails below top

Plan section @ lower shelf

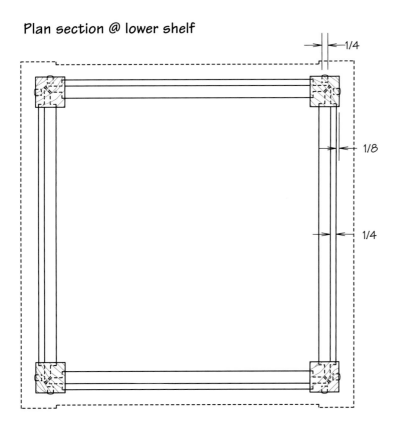

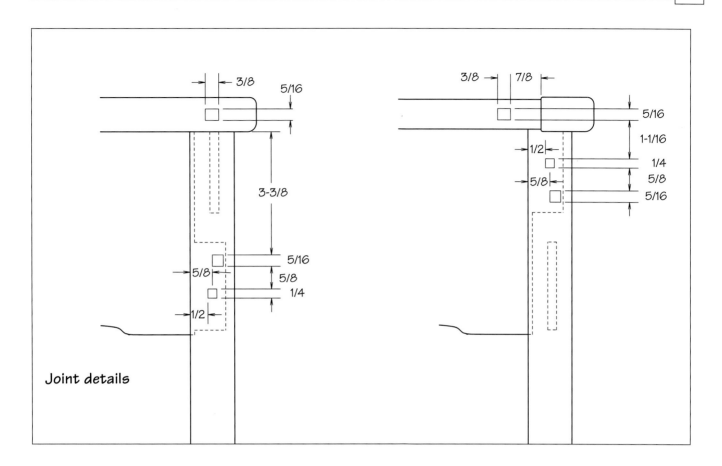

Joint details

Front elevation

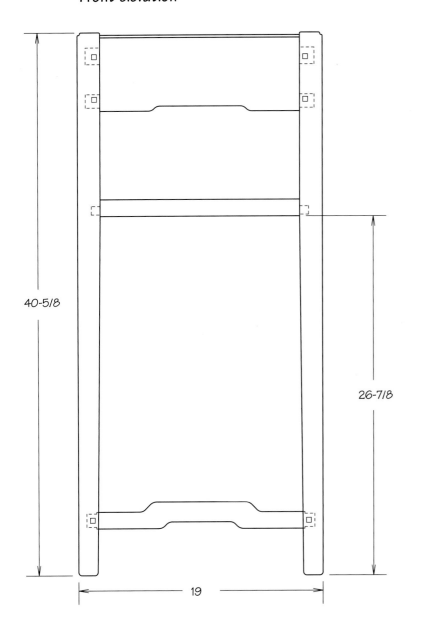

Side elevation

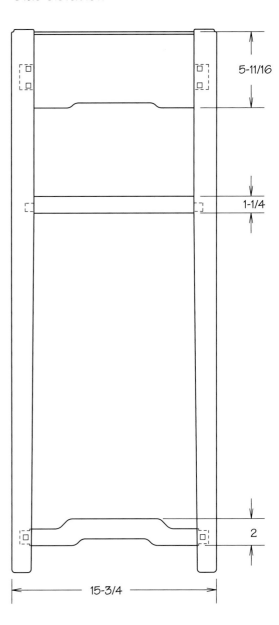

BOLTON PLANT STAND

As with the other Bolton/Bush pieces this mahogany stand has a very dark finish and a similar treatment at the top of the legs. The tenons on the top rails are arranged to pass each other where they would otherwise meet within the leg. This method allows for deeper tenons, which greatly add to the strength of the piece.

The cloud-lift stretchers are also offset, with the front higher off the floor than the sides. This integration of the design with the joinery details shows a clear understanding of structural matters on the part of the designer, or the ability of the craftsman making the piece to influence the design for the sake of structural integrity.

Front section

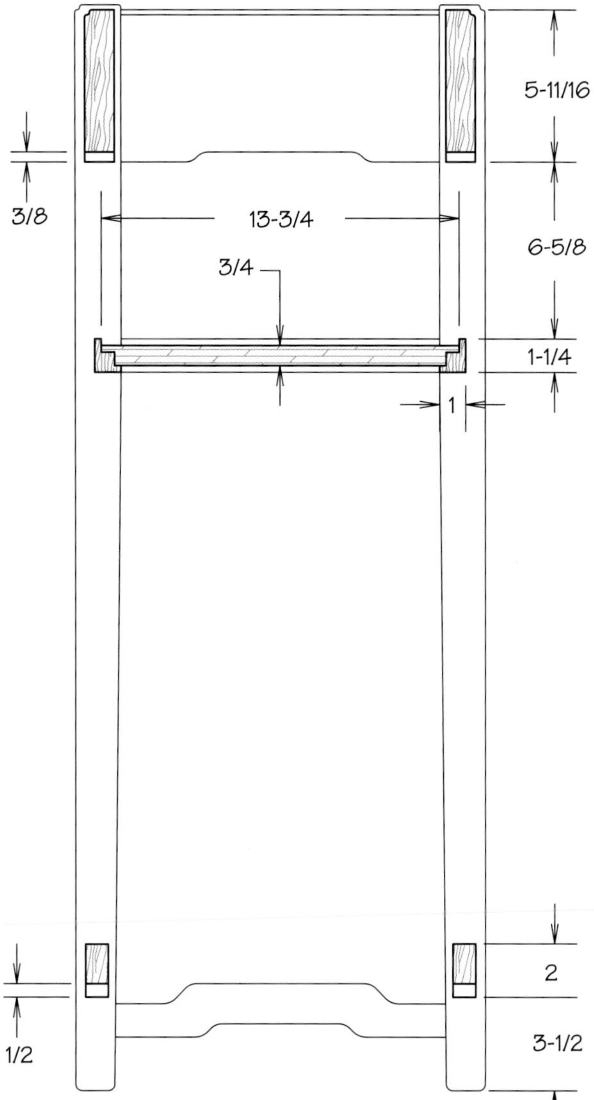

5-11/16

3/8

13-3/4

3/4

6-5/8

1-1/4

1

2

3-1/2

1/2

Side section

17

2

2

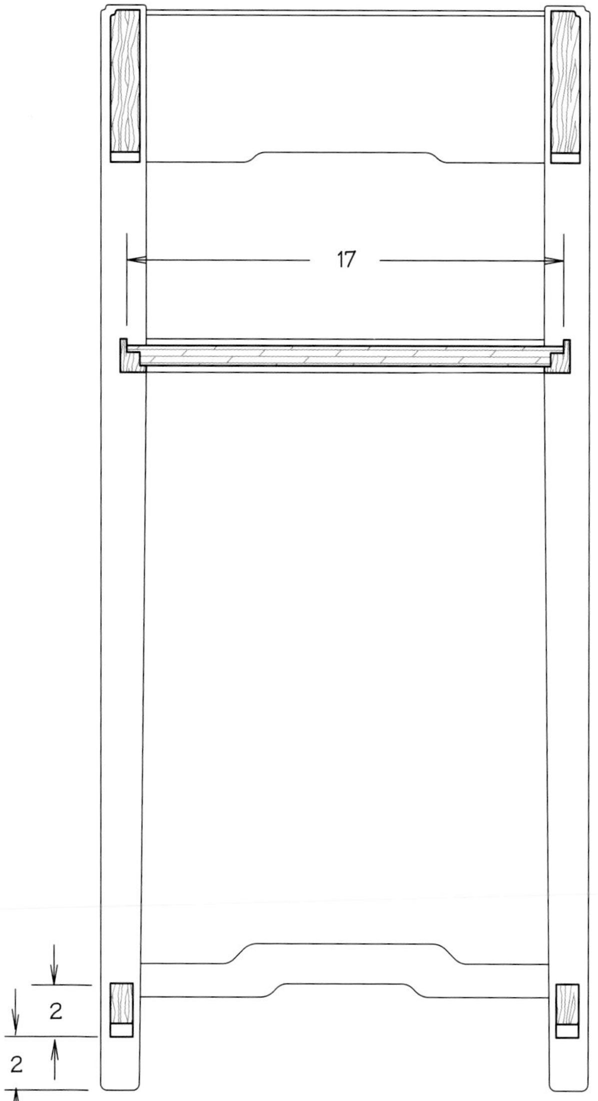

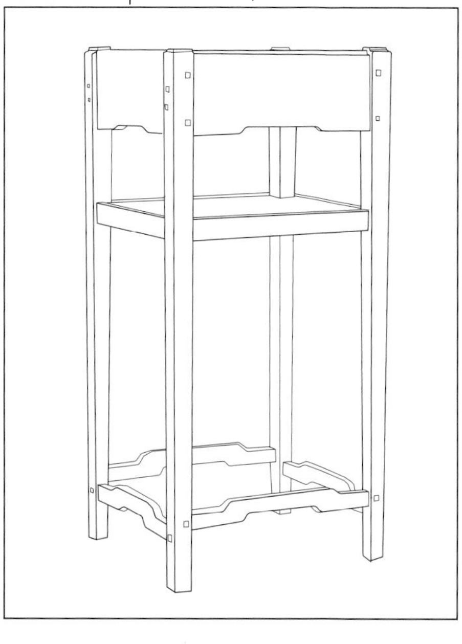

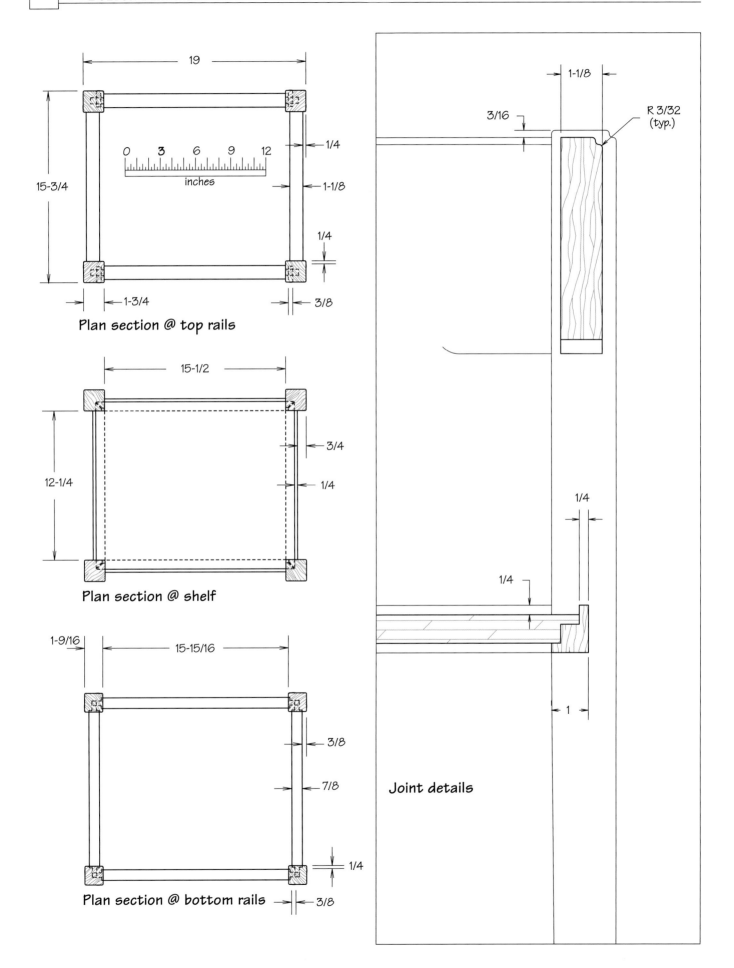

Plan section @ top rails

Plan section @ shelf

Plan section @ bottom rails

Joint details

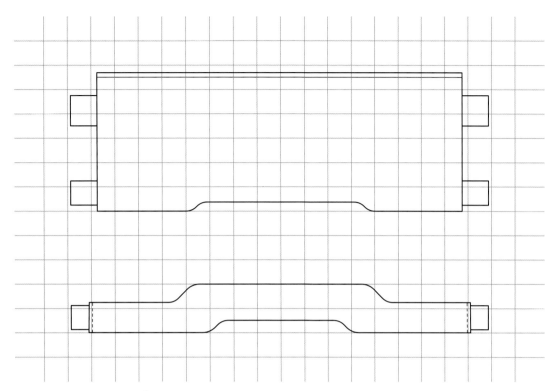

Front details grid = 1" squares

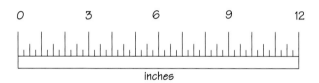

inches

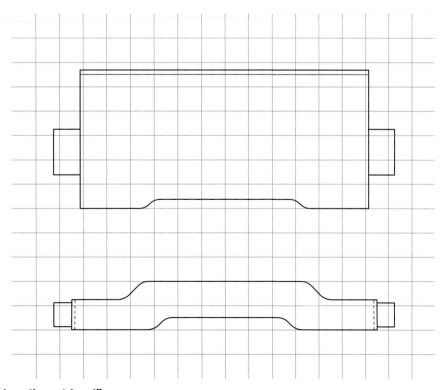

Side details grid = 1" squares

Blacker Night Stand

The original location of this piece is between two chairs in the bedroom of the Blacker House. It would also make an excellent bedside stand. The title on the archive drawing is "Mahogany Table for Bedroom #0". The original drawings indicate inlays on the tabletop, but in the existing piece, the inlays are described as on the breadboards in the "tree of life" pattern seen on some of the chairs in the house. I couldn't find a good photo of the inlays, or get a close look at the original so I did not include any inlays in my drawing.

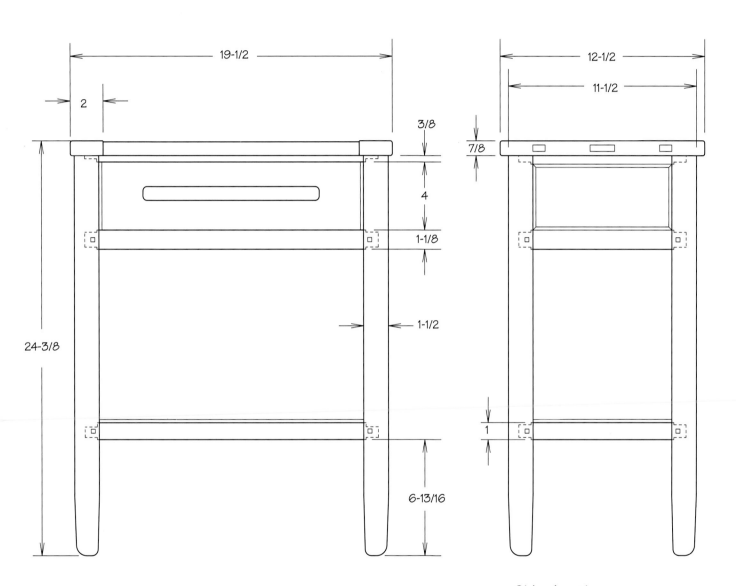

Front elevation

Side elevation

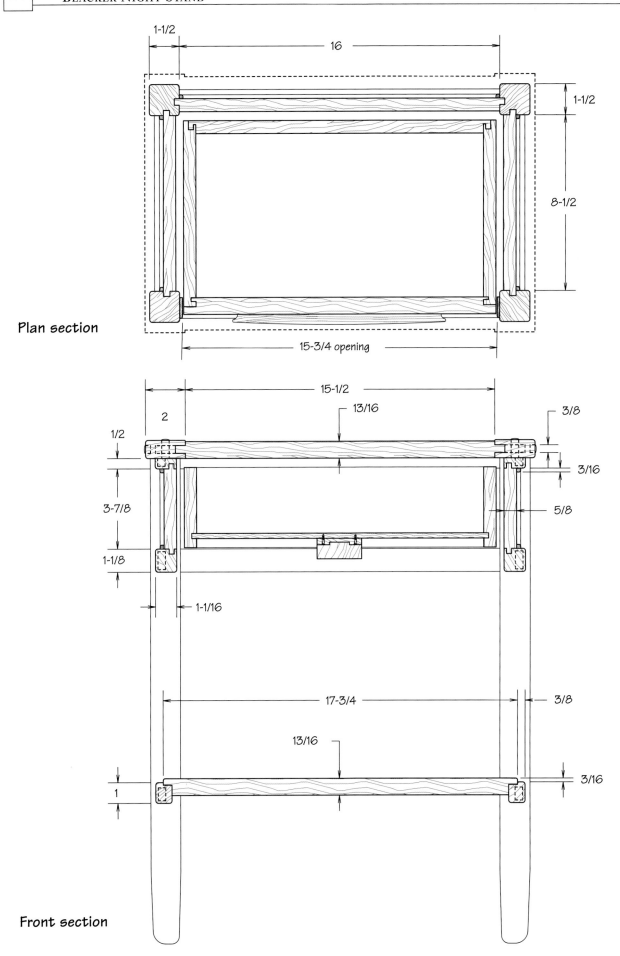

Plan section

Front section

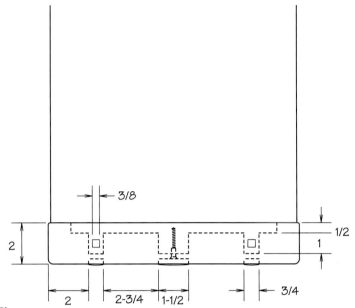

Plan

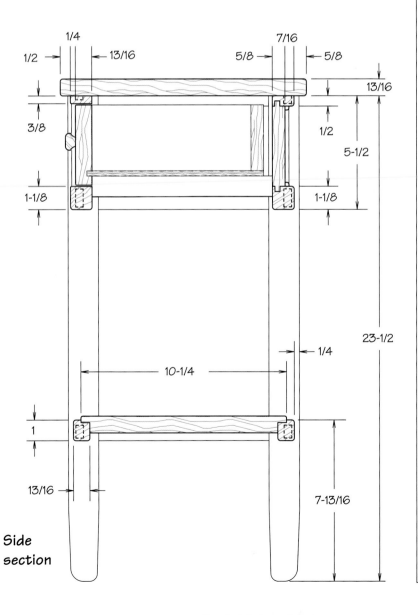

Side section

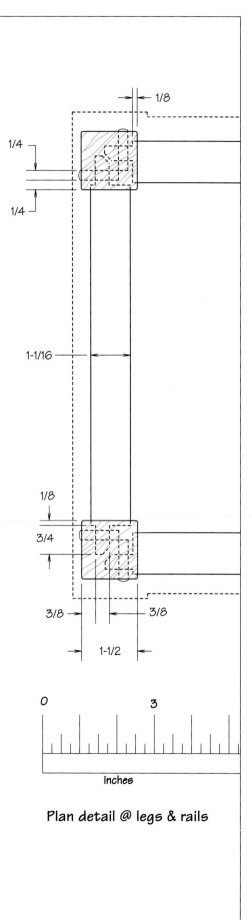

Plan detail @ legs & rails

Gamble House kitchen table

Photo: Ognan Borissov, Interfoto

GAMBLE KITCHEN TABLE

This large worktable in maple is the forerunner of today's kitchen island. The table is designed so that the drawers can be opened from either side, and the runners are made from oak to provide a longer wearing, smoother running surface. The top is a nice size for a work surface without being so large it dominates the room, and the open space under the drawers provides room to get under the table with a broom or mop to clean the floor.

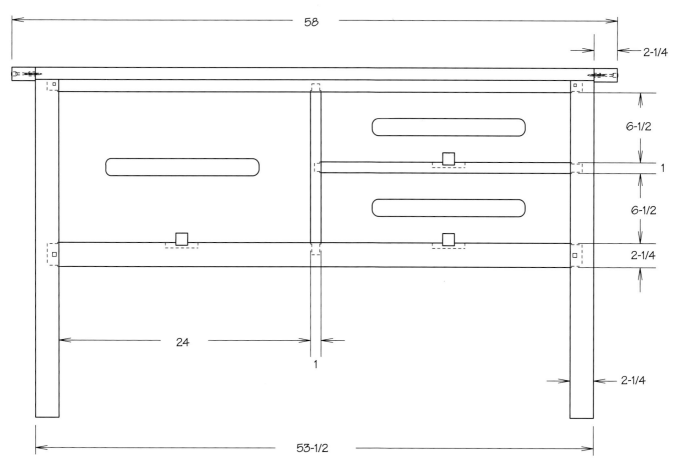

Front elevation

Front section

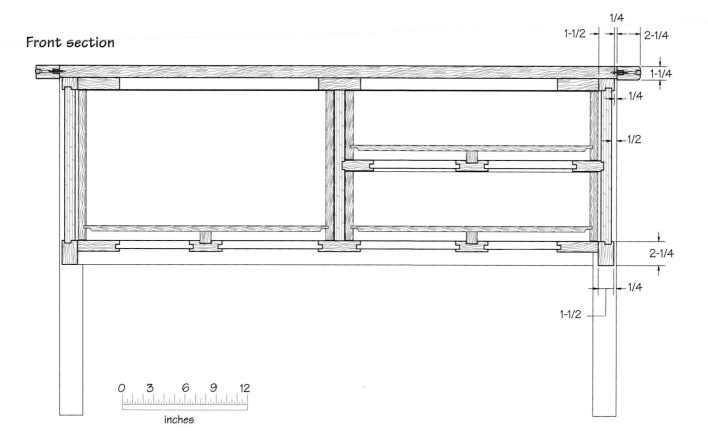

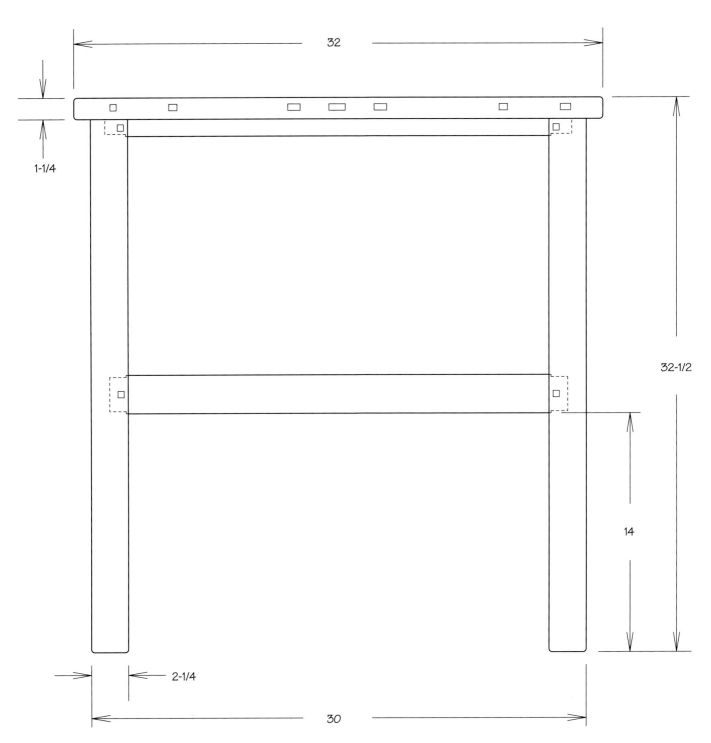

Side elevation

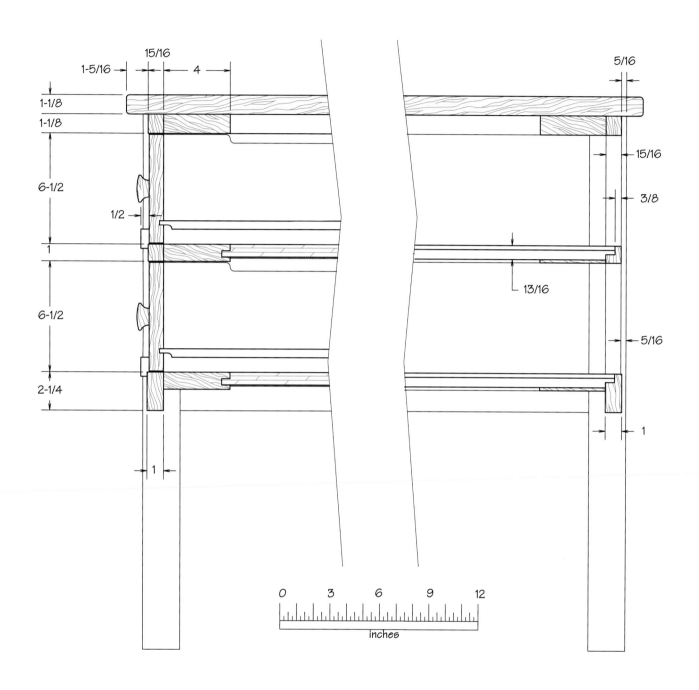

Side section with drawers

Side section with drawers removed

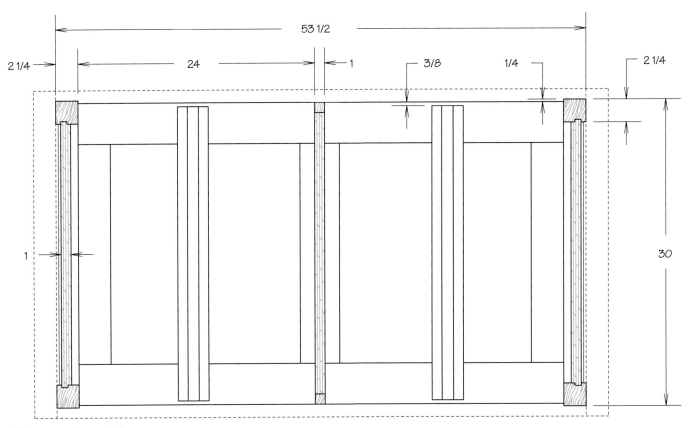

Plan section at top

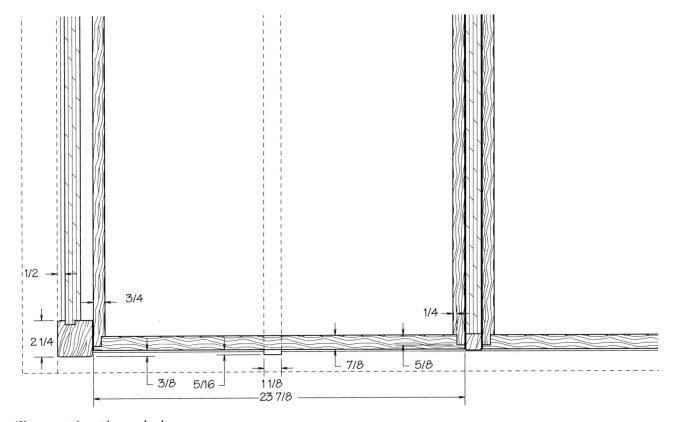

Plan section through drawer

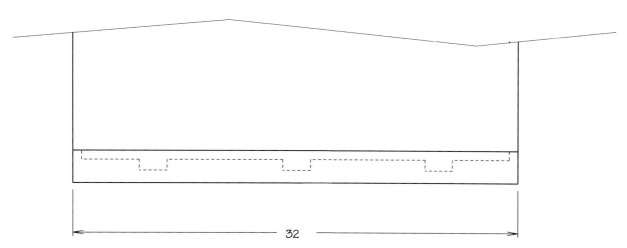

Breadboard end - plan

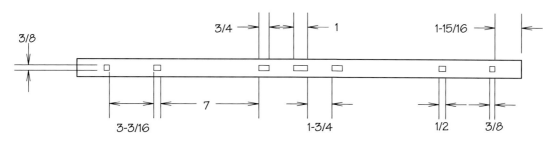

Breadboard end - elevation

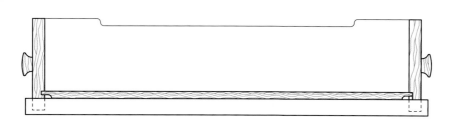

Side section through drawer

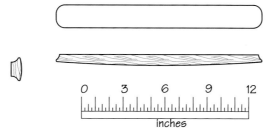

Handle detail

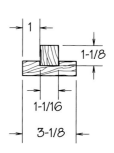

Drawer runner

Gamble House kitchen cabinets, now at the University of Southern California   Photo: Ognan Borissov, Interfoto

GAMBLE KITCHEN CABINETS

This is but one elevation of cabinets in the Gamble House kitchen. There is another, similar elevation on the adjacent wall, a free-standing three-drawer cabinet, and similar cabinets in the pantry off the kitchen. The biggest difference between the kitchen cabinets and the other built-ins and furniture in the home is the choice of wood, not the quality of workmanship. They are as nicely finished and detailed as any of the work in the home.

On concession made is in the joints of the drawers. The kitchen drawers have a simpler rabbet joint than the other furniture pieces. The upper cabinets have no backs, allowing the tile on the walls of the room to be seen through the glass doors.

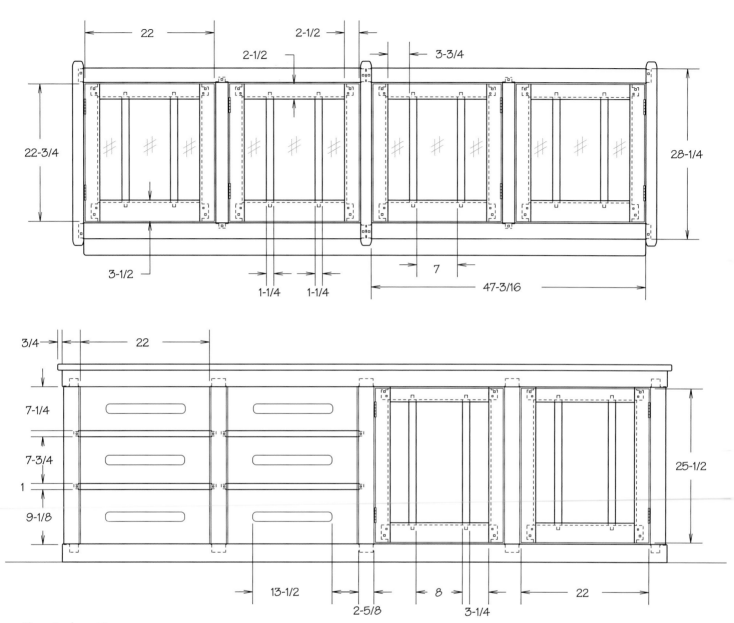

Front elevation

Side elevation

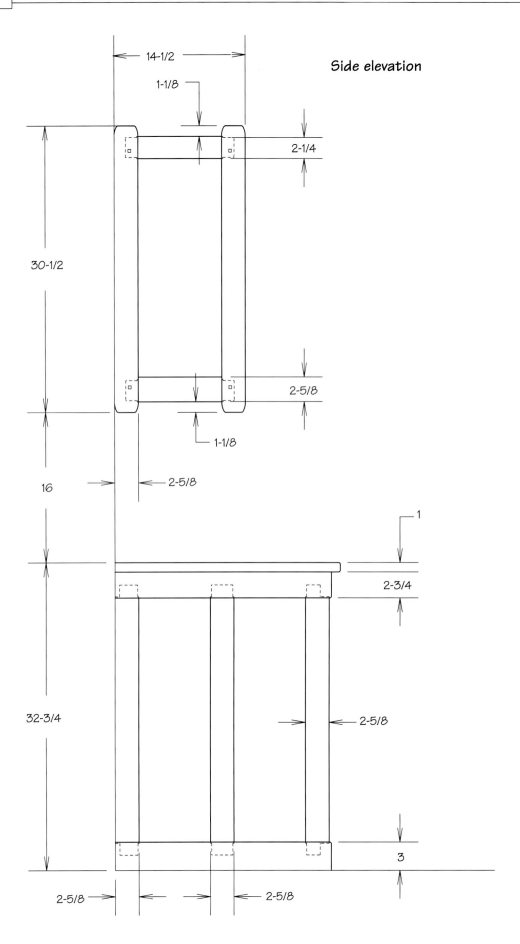

14-1/2

1-1/8

2-1/4

30-1/2

2-5/8

1-1/8

16

2-5/8

1

2-3/4

32-3/4

2-5/8

3

2-5/8

2-5/8

Side section

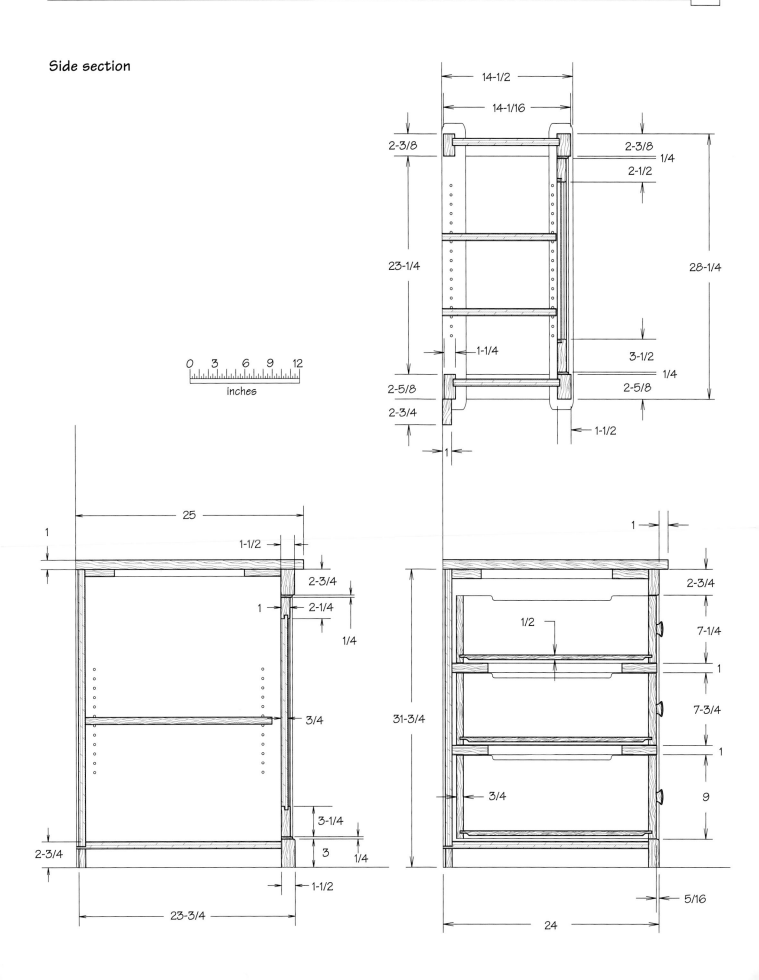

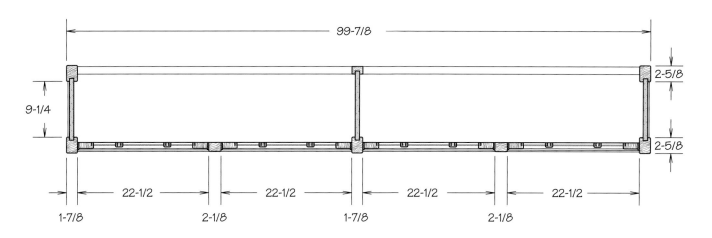

Plan section - upper cabinet

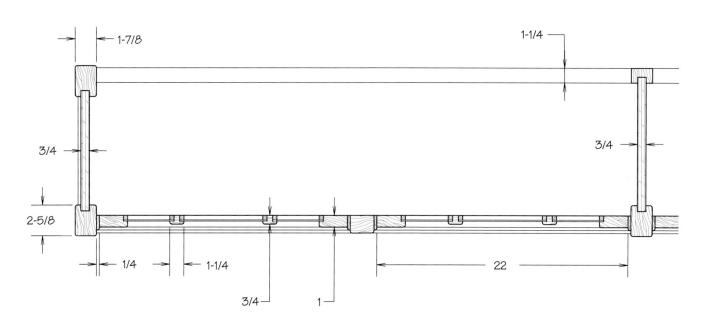

Plan detail @ glass doors

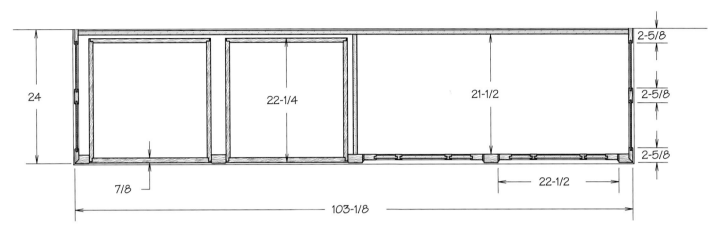

Plan section - base cabinet

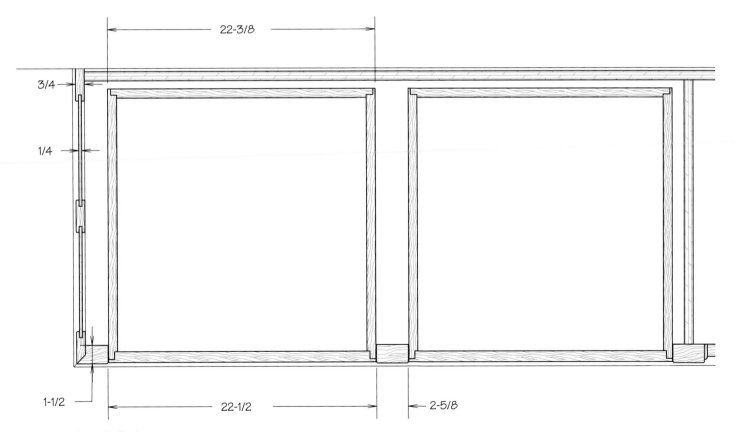

Plan detail @ drawers

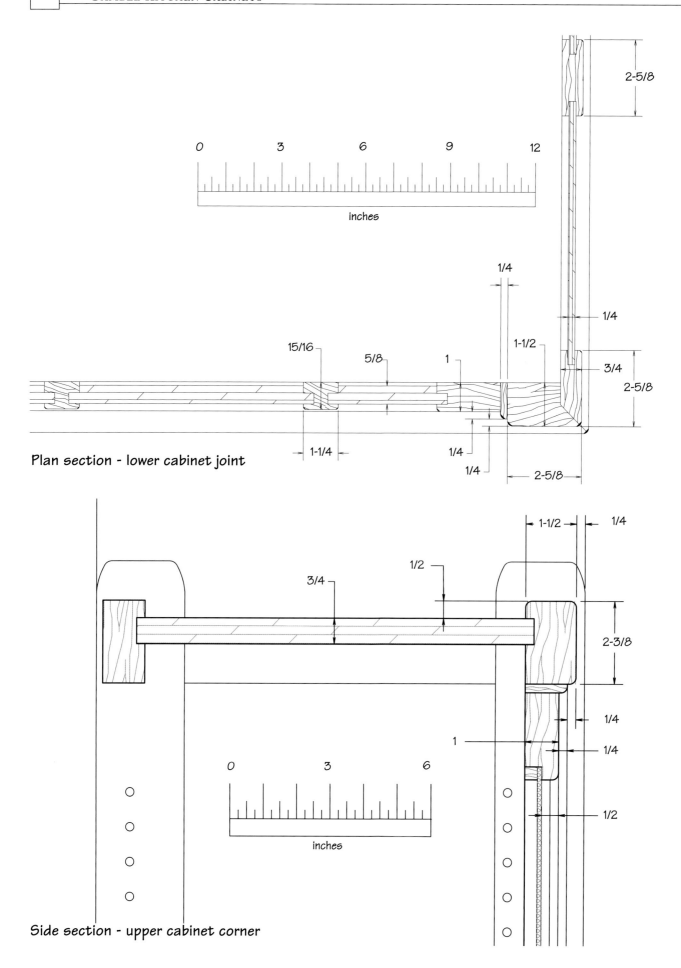

Plan section - lower cabinet joint

Side section - upper cabinet corner

CHARLES GREENE SIDEBOARD

This massive sideboard was commissioned by Charles Greene for his own home, and built by the Halls in 1913. This was just after the hectic years of the Ultimate Bungalow period, and it's interesting to see what the designer created when he was his own client. Most of the usual elements are present, but in a subtle, simplified form. The stepped front edges of the breadboards are the only detail that is more complex, but the ebony

pegs return to the earlier, rounded form.

It isn't known if these simplifications were to suit Charles Greene's taste or budget. He had several pieces made during this period, among the last of the furniture built for him and his clients by the Halls. Some were for his own home, but a rosewood chair and writing desk were put on display in a Pasadena store.

Plan

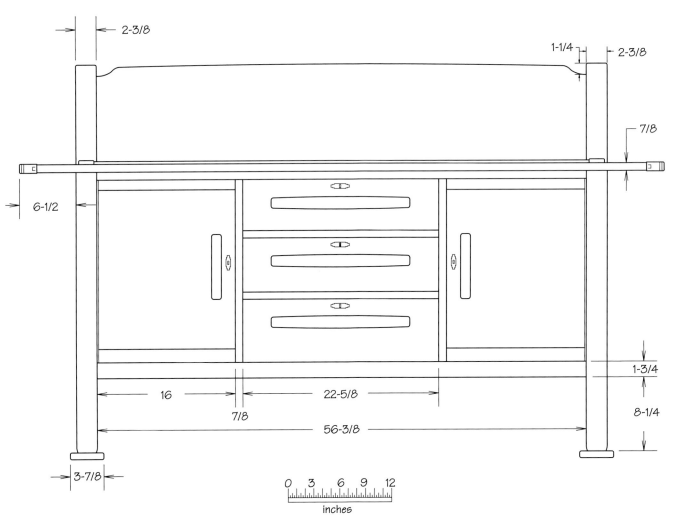

Front elevation

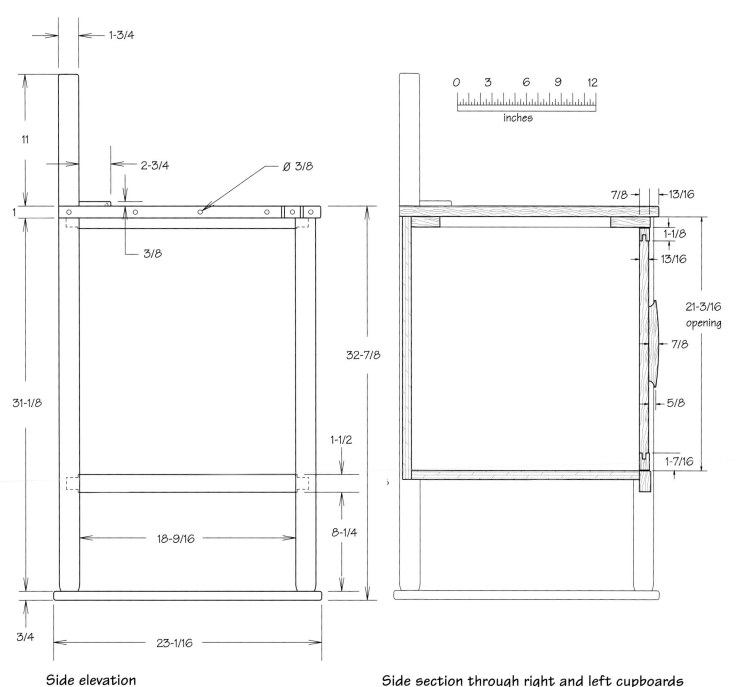

1-3/4

11

2-3/4

Ø 3/8

3/8

1

31-1/8

18-9/16

1-1/2

8-1/4

32-7/8

3/4

23-1/16

Side elevation

0   3   6   9   12

inches

7/8   13/16

1-1/8

13/16

21-3/16
opening

7/8

5/8

1-7/16

Side section through right and left cupboards

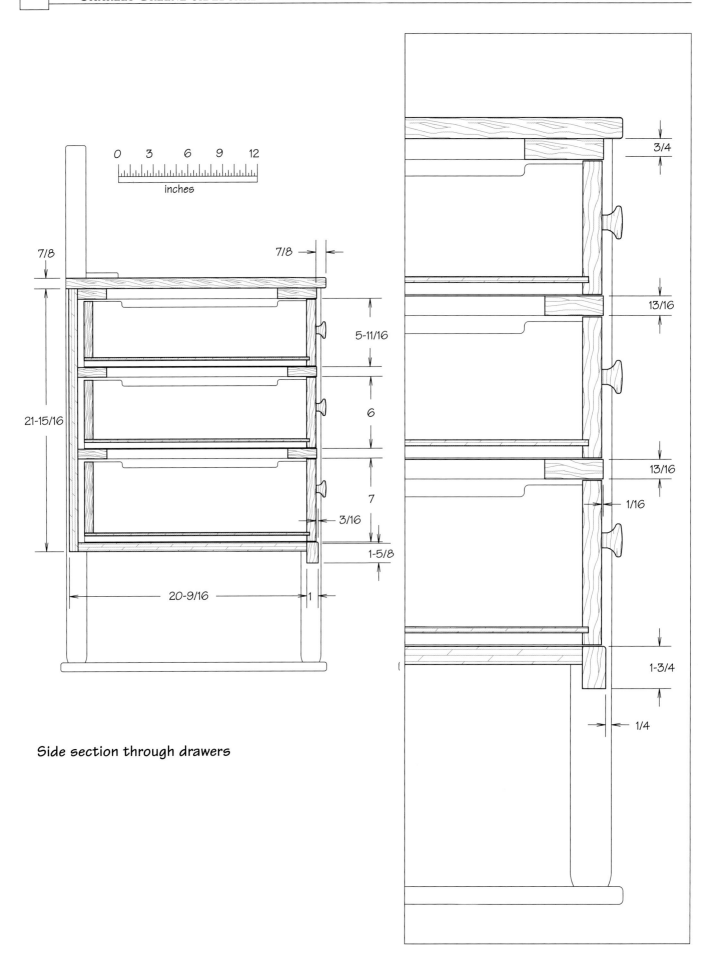

0   3   6   9   12

inches

7/8

7/8

5-11/16

21-15/16

6

7

3/16

1-5/8

20-9/16   1

Side section through drawers

3/4

13/16

13/16

1/16

1-3/4

1/4

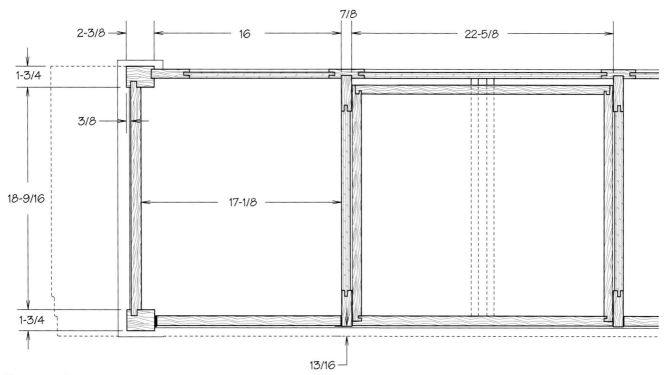

Plan section

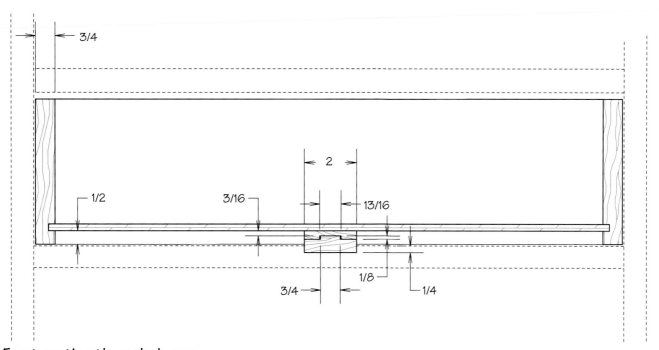

Front section through drawer

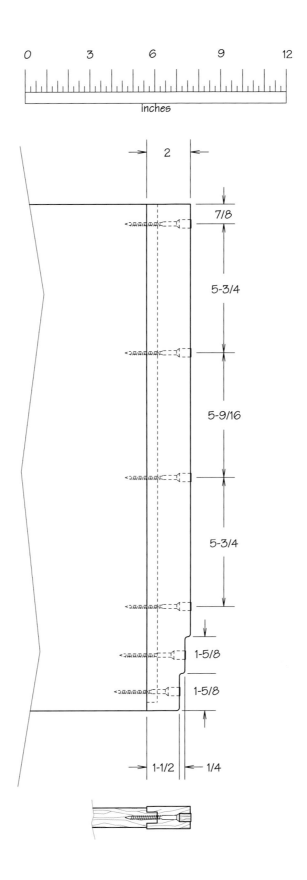

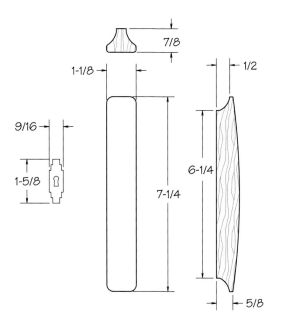

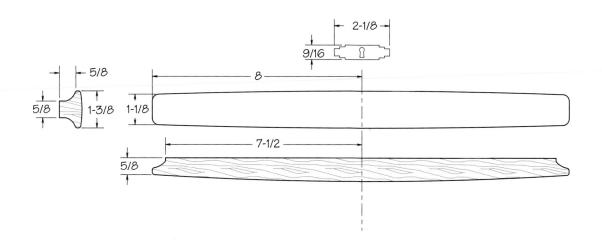

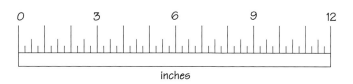

inches

Handle and escutcheon detail

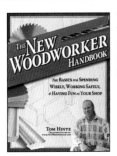

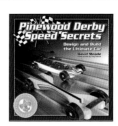